PEOPLE FIRST
ECONOMICS

PEOPLE FIRST
ECONOMICS

EDITED BY
David Ransom AND Vanessa Baird

WORLD
CHANGING

People First Economics

First published in the UK in 2009 by
New Internationalist™ Publications Ltd
Oxford OX4 1BW
www.newint.org
New Internationalist is a registered trademark.

Front cover and book design: Andrew Kokotka

Series editors: Troth Wells and Chris Brazier

 Printed on recycled paper by TJ International Limited, Cornwall, UK,
who hold environmental accreditation ISO 14001.

British Library Cataloguing-in-Publication Data.
A catalogue record for this book is available from the British Library.

Library of Congress Cataloguing-in-Publication Data.
A catalogue record for this book is available from the Library of Congress.

ISBN: 978-1-906523-23-7

Contents

Introduction

No-one who has been awake for the past two years could deny that the world has changed quite dramatically. The impacts of toxic debt, rising job losses, collapsing commodity prices and expanding poverty are being felt worldwide.

But the trillion-dollar question remains: will the deep transformations that are desperately needed be put into effect? Or will those people succeed who are determined to patch up a failing economic model and continue with 'business as usual' – business that suits the minority of the world's people at the ever-increasing expense of the majority?

The writers, thinkers and activists contributing to this book are not afraid of change. Each, in their way, sees in it a tremendous opportunity as well as a threat. They don't all agree on each detail of the way forward, but they are in agreement about one thing – we cannot go on like this.

So what? Even the most conservatively inclined politicians and analysts are making similar statements now. But the devil is in the detail. Commitments to cleaning up finance, tightening regulation, clamping down on the 'economics of greed', are apt to turn into the most modest tweaks that do little or nothing to stop the rot. Loudly trumpeted proposals signally fail to address the social and economic injustices that underpin the current economic system. The greater danger may not be change – but the lack of it.

The problems with the prevailing global economic system are well known to us at the *New Internationalist*. We have been writing about them for many years. Perhaps because our brief is to take a global perspective, especially from the point of view of the most disadvantaged in the Majority World, we have never been taken in by the 'globalization is good for you' pitch.

We know globalization has only been good for some people in some countries. For the vast majority, it has widened the gap between rich and poor, led to chronic under-employment and facilitated the plundering of natural resources by transnational corporations. Nobody knows more about the impact of debt than the peoples of the Global South; or about the way International Monetary Fund (IMF) conditions on loans have compounded poverty.

Today the IMF is once again a major player on the world stage – and once again there is one austere and punishing rule for the poor and another, much more lenient and accommodating, rule for the equally debt-ridden rich countries. Once again it is the most disadvantaged who are hit hardest.

We decided to call this book **People First Economics**, partly because *New Internationalist* has been involved in the Put People First coalition of civil society movements in Britain that are calling for social, economic and environmental justice. It should go without saying that economics should serve the needs of the people – not the other way around. But you could be forgiven for thinking that economics involves people being forced into some procrustean, mathematically defined framework – free-market liberalism, for example – simply because that's the way it's been for so many years.

The purpose of this book is unequivocally to shift the focus back to where we think it belongs – the needs of people and the environment. The two cannot be easily separated; nor should they be. At one point, while putting together this collection, we considered organizing it under separate headings such as 'economic', 'social', 'political' or 'environmental'. But we became increasingly aware that such an approach might be part of the problem, not part of the solutions we are aiming for.

So instead of artificial boundaries we have opted for a more fluid approach, involving cross-references within pieces so that you can, if you so choose, navigate your way down various streams of interest or concern. You can read this book progressively, from start to finish, or you can move around within it.

Taken together, we think these essays and articles suggest that another world is not just possible but essential, and already in the making.

David Ransom and **Vanessa Baird**
New Internationalist
Oxford

YASH
TANDON

BARBARA
EHRENREICH

JOHN
CHRISTENSEN

GEORGE
MONBIOT

PETER
STALKER

TAREK EL
DIWANY

The Age of Possibility

David Ransom reckons the meltdown could turn out to have made another world possible.

Given to us – perhaps once in a lifetime – is the chance, the responsibility, to see the world with fresh eyes. George Orwell described the fleeting, deceptive intoxication of such a moment in Barcelona in 1937. More recently, the people of Bolivia may well have felt it with the election of Evo Morales in 2005. There could even have been a trace of it in the US after Barack Obama's victory in 2008. On any given day, in a city or village somewhere in the world, people are probably experiencing something very similar for themselves. But never in my lifetime has everyone been forced to witness together the same spectacle – the meltdown of the world's financial 'architecture', the prison walls it built around us, the open space it leaves in front of us. Never have the possibilities, and the dangers, been so common or so great.

When jobs are being trashed and lives ruined, this may not be the most seemly moment to suggest that the meltdown might eventually prove to have been a good thing. But then, machines for the emission of carbon dioxide have been rusting pointlessly on airfields, and there's a chance for the skillful people who made them to make something much more useful – better, surely, than nothing at all. The meltdown, rather than interminable conferences, might actually have been cutting carbon emissions – in this crucial respect, the old regime worked only when it failed. Homes have become more affordable, just as people who need them get turfed out of them. Some people now find the growth of vital things like food more satisfying than 'economic growth' or losing oneself in a vacuous computer screen. A renewed sense of sufficiency, of the public interest and the common good, is being restored a little closer to its right place.

All the while, however, governments have been bending every sinew to put things back the way they were – the one mission that is, for all practical purposes, impossible.

In the space of a few months it became drearily commonplace to hear of, say, a handful of idiots on Wall Street paying themselves $20 billion from public funds as a reward for their inspired attempts to plunge the world into chaos. Even more characteristic of that world is the shameful fact that 80 in every 100 of their fellow human beings possess not so much as a single cent of social security; just 20 in every 100 consume 80 per cent and more of the world's vanishing resources. 'Money,' retorted one of those smart Wall Street fools by way of justification, 'is fungible' – raised for one purpose, it can legitimately be used for quite another. Let that, finally, be the epitaph for a misbegotten age.

I grew to maturity through the 1960s and 1970s in Europe and Latin America, when power was being ceded to financial markets. How it had been possible, in a society bankrupted by war at the time, to establish the National Health Service in Britain and bring key sectors of the economy under some sort of democratic control (including, in 1946, the Bank of England itself), was already hard to imagine.

The merest hint of an offense against financial markets

became, by 1979 and the election of Margaret Thatcher, enough to send political parties of all shades running for 'realism'. By the 1990s, a prospective New Labour government was charting its path to power through 'prawn cocktail offensives' in the City of London franchise of Wall Street, and around the tropical tax havens of Rupert Murdoch. Plenty of people bought in to the myopic realism of it all. Relatively few foresaw that Tony Blair would eventually find fulfillment as the most expensive after-dinner warbler in the world. Gordon Brown's first public act as Prime Minister was to invite Margaret Thatcher to tea. By January 2009, at a uniquely somber World Economic Forum in Davos, Switzerland, the would-be savior of the world pronounced himself quite at ease without the slightest idea where events were leading him.

Quite suddenly, it is the realists who no longer know what they are 'for' – Thatcher's 'moaning minnies' who do. Though you would never have guessed it from the corporate media, at exactly the same time as Davos but in Belém, Brazil, the World Social Forum was under way. Perhaps 100,000 people from social movements around the world gathered at the mouth of the Amazon to gain strength from each other and debate the fate of the environment, the irresistible urge for social justice, human dignity, survival itself. The Forum's motto is: 'Another World is Possible'. If, at the beginning of 2009, the nabobs of Davos already seemed to personify the past, Belém offered another glimpse into a future that might actually be worth having.

Cynics dismiss the Forum – if they consider it at all – as a dream factory. It doesn't behave like a proper political party, deploying disciplined cadres and huge quantities of compromising cash on propaganda campaigns. It doesn't aim to make apathy the prevailing popular mood. It has its own reluctant seers, like Eduardo Galeano, but prefers to dwell on diversity rather than orthodoxy. Heaven forfend, ancient terms like 'socialism' are quite common currency. To some people that looks, well really, a bit flaky.

How odd, then, that not just one but five hard-nosed Presidents showed up together in Belém: Evo Morales (a former coca grower) from Bolivia, Hugo Chávez (a former soldier) from Venezuela, Fernando Luco (a former Catholic bishop) from Paraguay, Rafael Correa (an economist trained in Chicago, of all places) from Ecuador and Lula da Silva (a former car worker and union organizer) from Brazil. Naturally, they had their own motives for being there, their own varied records to defend. But, as Fernando Luco pointed out, some of them had been to previous Forums, before they became Presidents. 'If we are Presidents today,' said Morales, 'we owe it to you.' 'Ten years ago,' said Chávez, 'an encounter between five Presidents of the region and their social movements would have been unthinkable.'

Who, then, can be entirely sure of what is or is not thinkable anywhere else? One does not have to ignore the limitations of what is happening in Latin America, or revert to wishful thinking about this least romantic of continents, to suggest that if such a thing can happen here then other possibilities are at least thinkable almost anywhere.

Like most people, I reckon, my own sense of what is possible stems from what I already know to be so. For 20 years and until quite recently, I worked at the New Internationalist in Oxford, a workers' co-operative. This may sound idealistic to you, but I found it quite practical, because that's what co-operation is. Ideals still had a place, but someone who wished to live on ideals alone, free from human frailty, wouldn't have been satisfied for long. We had a turnover of a few million dollars each year without recourse to a greasy pole or a CEO. No-one could tell anyone else what to do – we were all paid the same, perfectly sufficient living wage. We played no financial instruments and offered no 'incentives' of the kind that banks seem to believe are the only thing worth working for. We relied for support not on advertisers or the ego of a mogul, but on our subscribers. As a result, we had no-one but ourselves to blame for our shortcomings. Even so, I reckon our co-op worked a good deal better than the banks. I find it hard to imagine how anyone in their right mind would ever wish to work in any other way, though I know full well that most people still must.

This experience suggests to me that the most durable (though by no means infallible) decisions, at work as much as anywhere else, are reached by informed discussion between people who thereby come to share a sense of responsibility for them – not by handing them over to someone else. That sense, which can be perverse as well as inspired, lives in the guts of a much-falsified idea: democracy. How it might best be realized is never more than a rather muddled, sometimes laborious form of work in progress. But it does provide a clear and constant appreciation of what progress actually is, not least when orthodoxy evaporates into the thin air it came from.

So it's not just by chance that we failed to be dazzled by consumer culture and corporate globalization. Sadly, the same cannot often be said of those who now claim to be working on our behalf, most recently through the G20.

This hybrid group of the world's 20 grandest national economies, which includes 'emerging' countries like China, India and Brazil, appears to be supplanting the rich club of the G7/8, at least when it comes to the global meltdown. Not merely are some of these countries (China, Saudi Arabia) the only ones with trade surpluses and appetizing 'sovereign wealth' funds at their disposal. They also need to be implicated in the status quo – to the exclusion of the rest of the world, and of the one legitimate global body we do have, which is the UN.

The G20 summit in London on 2 April 2009 was met on the previous weekend by a large demonstration from an almost unprecedented alliance, across social and environmental divides, of some 160 movements in Britain – as well as by 'direct action' in London's financial district, despite a severe crackdown by an increasingly menacing police force.

The summit of largely bewildered leaders went some way towards the inescapable conclusion that free-market neoliberalism is shipwrecked, while the 'hidden hand' of financial markets had been in the till all along. So there was apparent agreement on more financial regulation, fewer tax havens and a lot more cash for poor countries – ironically enough, precisely those that had been excluded from the G20 itself.

Unfortunately, the G20 is a 'virtual' group confronting a meltdown that is all too material. There's no effective mechanism for regulating the global financial system – and, seemingly, no awareness that regulation is not a technical fix but an act of democratic control. Tax havens (like Britain) can be 'named and shamed' as much as the G20 may like, but shame is no substitute for the simple act of removing legal recognition from their accounts. As for the 'trillion dollars' that were promised for the poorest countries, a goodly chunk was apparently to come from China, which denied all knowledge as soon as the summit was over. Funny money for a virtual world, indeed.

Out of mere instinct, the G20 is still trying to rebuild the very financial architecture that has collapsed, including the Unholy Trinity of 'multilateral' institutions that were its caretakers. Together, the International Monetary Fund, World Bank and World Trade Organization have failed no less completely than the private banks they mimicked, and whose interests they ultimately served. Chancellor Angela Merkel of Germany whispered support for making them accountable to an Economic Council at the UN – a tentative step back towards a structure from which all three of the Unholy Trinity were quite unscrupulously severed at birth. More ominously for the status quo, Russia and China began to talk of replacing the US dollar as the international 'reserve' currency, perhaps by reverting to gold. Even these retrogressive notions proved too material for the G20.

What it did manage to agree on could well prove less significant than what it didn't. In particular, the London summit marked the end of 'fiscal stimulus' – the notion that, having bailed out the banks, governments should now do something to help their victims. Nothing will happen as a result of the G20 that does not go through the collapsed financial architecture – and the signs already are that at least some private banks, now merged into near-monopolies, will make yet another killing as a result. All that remains for everyone else is the prospect of unemployment, tax hikes and public-service cuts. And for what? It was left to US President Barack Obama to place a fig leaf over the proceedings and promise that the G20 would 'go on trying until we get it right'. Both he and we could have a long wait coming.

Better, surely, to make a clean start. In order to do this, further difficulties will have to be overcome.

The most immediate is that the G20 made not so much as a gesture towards the complexity of the meltdown; financial, social, environmental and, arguably, political as well.

The thinking seemed to be that 'climate' could be consigned to the Copenhagen conference in December 2009. There was no attempt to link the way forward to the massive investment that is urgently required in 'green' jobs, or to ways of reducing carbon emissions other than by market-based 'carbon trading', which is already a useless fiasco. The run-up to Copenhagen was thereby doomed to focus on the absence of cash – we can afford only to kill the planet.

Yet the unthinkable has already happened. General Motors is bankrupt, Toyota has made the first loss in its history. Transnational corporations have been as deeply implicated in financial speculation as the banks. It is unlikely that a corporate meltdown would be confined to General Motors. Meanwhile, an unquantifiable stack of 'toxic debts' still lurk in the financial cesspit, waiting to make their next call on the taxpayer. How long before governments go bankrupt as well?

Here the question of political will becomes crucial. Deciding to bail out the private banks with public money is, after all, an act of political will. It is no less so to deny public assistance to anyone else. But, thus far and for the most part, the world's people have been mere passive spectators. There can be no durable solution without their active participation.

The problem that six or seven billion people will always have in reaching or expressing a common sense of democratic responsibility has no obvious solution. Indeed, corporate globalization flourished precisely because there isn't one. Nevertheless, global economic meltdown and climate change mean that progress towards one becomes increasingly vital.

Then again, corporate globalization was once said to presage the demise of the nation-state. Yet the nation-state remains just about the only institution with effective tax-raising powers, for the simple reason that it comes closest – if not necessarily that close – to democratic legitimacy. Tax-payers' funds have now been requisitioned to bail out corporate globalization, without for the most part any sort of democratic mandate at all.

The best answer we're ever likely to get is emerging, I am quite sure, from the bottom up, not from the top down – from Belém rather than from Davos; from villages and municipalities rather than from nation-states; from workplaces and homes that are occupied rather than vacant; from the resistance that mounts as the self-propelled meltdown careers along its wayward path; from wherever the sense of democratic responsibility can best be expressed.

Great areas of debate will doubtless remain. Markets may have their place but, unhinged as they have become from human cultures, they have lost any sense of where that might be. The day someone stands for election in a relatively rich country, says 'vote for me and consume less stuff' and gets elected, will be the day liberal democracy has a future. That could be the same day we conclude that $15 trillion spirited from nowhere to sustain financial markets might better have been spent on almost anything else; that the force of arms is helpless against the force of nature; that progress gained by the few at the expense of the rest is no progress at all. The Age of Possibility would then truly be upon us.

David Ransom was a *New Internationalist* co-editor from 1989 to 2009.

Connections: Naomi Klein, p 45; Walden Bello, p 57; Evo Morales, p 165; Michael Albert, p 169; Derek Wall, p 181; John Hilary p 217.

RICHARD
WILKINSON &
KATE PICKETT

YASH
TANDON

BARBARA
EHRENREICH

JOHN
CHRISTENSEN

GEORGE
MONBIOT

PETER
STALKER

DI

VANESSA BAIRD
WALDEN BELLO
SUSAN GEORGE
NAOMI KLEIN
NOAM CHOMSKY
ANN PETTIFOR

Beyond the Crash – a Green New Deal

Ann Pettifor was one of the first to predict the crash. Now she points to a sustainable way out of it.

The world is now faced by a terrifying prospect: large scale, systemic and long-term economic failure of a liberalized, highly integrated economy. This crisis – benignly named the Credit Crunch – is caused by the bursting of a massive bubble of privately created credit, issued at high real rates of interest, which has become unrepayable.

Credit in turn inflated asset bubbles, including bubbles in property, stocks and shares, brands, works of art, vintage cars, and commodities like oil, grains and gold.[1]

Assets are on the whole owned by the rich, and so inflation in the value of assets was a major reason for the rich growing richer over the last three decades. Furthermore the rich do not need to engage in *productive activity*, and instead can collect rent from their assets – whether in the form of returns on property, dividends from stocks and shares, rent from the intellectual property on brands, or gains from the sale of works of art.

Those engaged in productive activity – the owners of small businesses, farms or companies, the waged and middle classes –

have not enjoyed a parallel inflation of prices for their goods and services, or of wages or salaries.

They have therefore had to borrow to invest in their businesses, or to pay for a roof over their heads, or to send their children to university, or just to stay afloat. They are now burdened by debts, which soon become unpayable with rises in the rate of interest, or because of the shock of bankruptcy or unemployment. The first to fall victim to this process on a large scale were the 'sub-prime' debtors of the United States. But the debt dominoes are falling all over the Anglo-American economies, in Asia and in Europe – particularly eastern Europe.

Defaults and arrears on debts damaged the balance sheets of banks and precipitated the Credit Crunch of August 2007. Losses and liabilities were hidden behind complex financial products and this led to the evaporation of trust between banks. Inter-bank lending froze, and so central banks were forced to pump $150 billion of liquidity into the financial system to keep it functioning. Defaults led to major bank failures and losses – notably the collapse of Northern Rock in Britain and Bear Stearns in the United States, as well as the bankruptcy of Lehman's Bank – and to the write-off of hundreds of billions of dollars of debt. This in turn caused banks to cut back on new lending, and to raise interest rates on loans.

High borrowing costs on a heavy overhang of debt forced many companies into laying off workers and/or bankruptcy. Unemployment in all the world's economies began to spiral.

Unemployment is a key determinant of the ability to repay debts. As companies found it difficult to borrow, and as borrowing costs for new and existing loans remained high for companies engaged in any risky economic activity, there were further rises in bankruptcies and job losses. Unless action is taken to lower borrowing costs, and place a floor under falls in asset prices (like property) we can expect wave after wave of company and mortgage defaults, leading to higher unemployment and, with it, deeper, more systemic banking crises.

The ease with which credit can be created (unlike the struggles faced by those who work productively to create products and services from land or labor) has inflated the value of *assets*. Too much credit chasing too few *assets* inflates the value of assets. This is nowhere more obvious than in British house prices, which rose by 150 per cent between 1996 and 2006.

Remember also that while we may all have access to money, in the form of wages, pensions or benefits, not all of us have access to *credit*. Only those with existing assets – property, for example – can borrow against those assets. Those without assets have to take on huge risks, pay loan sharks exorbitant rates of interest for 'unsecured credit' – or go without. At the same time, wage growth has been tamed by the economic policies that underpinned globalization.

It is easy to understand how this system has helped the rich become richer while the rest have become poorer – and more indebted. And why in Britain, for example, the assets of the wealthy have increased 317 per cent during 11 years of New Labour rule.

Orthodox economists, particularly those with 'inflation-phobia', never complain about the inflation of assets; nor do economic commentators in the financial press. Neither do orthodox economists take money or credit into account, when considering prices of property, for example. Instead the theory of 'supply and demand' is dominant.

Economists let it be known in the 1980s and 1990s that rises in property prices had little to do with an excess supply of credit, but were a 'natural' result of the 'supply and demand' for housing. All kinds of theories were developed to explain this increase in demand: higher divorce rates, atomized families; and increased migration. However the weakness of the 'supply and demand' theory became evident in 2007 in the US, when credit tightened and – though divorce rates remained high, families stayed atomized and immigrants still entered the country – demand for housing fell precipitously.

Central bank governors and finance ministers regularly rail against the threat of inflation in wages and prices, even though this threat continues to elude them as core inflation remains very low. The recent spike in energy and food prices, caused in part by 'peak oil', by an increase in demand from China, but also by a wall of speculative money moving out of property and into commodities, has, at the time of writing, failed to lift wage inflation.

Prices worldwide have been falling. The cause of these falling prices lies with the de-leveraging of debts in rich countries, and with policies pursued by countries like China.

Enormous productive capacity has been created in China over the last two decades, at rates of growth unprecedented in history. Thousands of factories have been built and millions of workers employed to feed the demand from rich countries for low-cost goods and services. Some estimate that 40 per cent of Chinese GDP is dedicated to the production of exports for rich countries. A large proportion of China's greenhouse gas emissions are due to its role as manufacturer for consumers in the West.

Now, as the financial crisis in rich countries deepens, and as demand for imports from China falls, so the factories and workers of China are becoming idle. Despite its large population, Chinese consumption alone ($1 trillion) is still too low to compensate for a fall in demand from far bigger consumers, like the US ($9 trillion) and the EU.

Excess capacity, idle factories and workers in China will place downward pressure on wages and prices worldwide. Such downward pressure is known as deflation. The deflation of prices and wages hurts the providers and producers of goods and services. As profits and incomes are squeezed by falling prices, so companies go to the wall and unemployment rises.

If falling prices of goods and services are amplified by the rise of debts and the deflation of assets, then whole economies can quickly spiral downwards in a debt-deflationary tailspin.

As the Credit Crunch took hold after the events of August 2007, central bank governors succumbed to demands from the banking sector immediately to lower official interest rates. The European Central Bank remained the exception, and to widespread dismay, raised interest rates in July 2008 – just as the crisis was deepening.

US interest rates have since fallen almost to zero. These cuts in *official* interest rates pleased and cheered stock markets, which powered onwards and upwards in the expectation that the 'sorcerers' at the Federal Reserve could keep the credit bubble afloat.

However, at the same time privately fixed interest rates continued to rise, in defiance of *official* rates, set by central banks. This was the clearest evidence of central banks and governments losing control over a key lever of the economy – the power to set the rate of interest over all loans whether short, long, safe or risky. Indeed Alan Greenspan, former chair of the US Federal Reserve, admitted as much in the *Financial Times* on 5 August 2008. 'Since early this decade,' he wrote, 'central banks *have had to* cede control of long-term interest rates to global market forces' (my italics).

These invisible and unaccountable global market forces did their work. The ratcheting upwards of interest rates as the debt crisis took hold exacerbated the crisis by bankrupting individual and corporate debtors and caused severe damage to bank balance sheets, forcing them to write down debts and raise billions of fresh capital.

Warren Buffet, CEO of Berkshire Hathaway, in his letter to shareholders on 27 February 2009, wrote: 'Though Berkshire's credit is pristine – we are one of only seven AAA corporations in the country – our cost of borrowing is now far *higher* than competitors with shaky balance sheets but government backing.'

The guardians of the nation's finances in economies across the world had ceded control over one of the most important levers of the economy, one that determines the cost of debts, the gains to be made by lenders, and the ability of borrowers to repay. Above all, this is a lever that could help economies recover from large-scale economic failure – if only their central bank governors were willing to consider reclaiming this enormous power from a reckless private sector.

The rate of interest is a social construct, not a product of market forces. By ceding control over rates, central bankers had raised their hands in surrender, abandoning the helm of the ship that is the economy and with it millions of innocent victims of the crisis.

The massive deflation/de-leveraging of credit and debt that is now cascading through the banking systems of all the Organization of Economic Co-operation and Development (OECD) – or rich – countries is rapidly deflating the value of housing and other assets in these economies and will exacerbate large-scale, global economic failure. This will not be a 'failure of substance. We are stricken by no plague of locusts,' to quote Franklin D Roosevelt.[2] Instead we are stricken by the consequences of decisions by Anglo-American central bank governors and finance ministers to abandon their duty to act as guardians of the nation's finances and instead to deregulate financial systems and give free rein to the private finance sector to engage in reckless, destabilizing, irresponsible, unethical, and often fraudulent actions.

The tragedy is that our predicament is the result of ignoring, denying and even concealing lessons known to our predecessors, especially those that dealt with the Credit Crunch of the 1920s and 1930s. The most important of these lessons is that the interests of the private financial sector are opposed to the interests of society as a whole, and therefore have to be carefully regulated by bodies accountable to the public.

This is the context in which a small group of economists (including this author), industrialists and a banker designed and launched the Green New Deal in association with the London-based New Economics Foundation in July 2008.

The Green New Deal recognizes that the world is facing a triple crunch: a severe and prolonged financial crisis, peak oil and climate change. We propose policies to deal with all three 'crunches' – and acknowledge that they cannot be addressed separately or sequentially.

Under the Green New Deal we propose first, that in order to salvage the global financial system it will be vital to declare a Grand Jubilee of debt cancellation. This will enable debtors to write off unpayable debts and to allow banks to restore their balance sheets to health.

Such a proposal might well prove unpalatable to financial institutions. The only alternative then, if we are to salvage the financial system, is to raise the incomes of those that must repay debts. The policies of governments determined to hold down incomes as the debt crisis accelerates poses a fundamental threat to the interests of, for example, Wall Street or the City of London. Mervyn King, the Governor of the Bank of England, in his June 2008 Mansion House speech, warned that mean real take-home pay would stagnate, and the squeeze on real income growth will likely mean that both house prices and consumer spending weaken together. But it will also mean an increase in debt defaults.

The situation is already urgent in the US, where the phenomenon of 'jingle post' has emerged. The implicit social contract that ensures debtors have sufficient income to repay debts has broken down, and so debtors are taking matters into their own hands. Unable to repay their mortgages, increase their incomes or secure their jobs, they simply pop the keys of their property into the post, return it to the bank, and walk away from their debts. As the scale of these defaults rise, so the authorities lose control over the enforcement of debt payments. Only when a new social contract is established, either through debt cancellation or through higher incomes for debtors, can we expect the financial system to be restored to stability.

Infusions of liquidity and bail-outs of bank managers and shareholders have not succeeded in stalling the financial crisis. A more radical approach is needed, and for this politicians and economists need the intellectual courage and rigor demonstrated by leaders like Keynes and Roosevelt, who challenged the finance sector, subordinated it to the interests of society as a whole, and helped drag western economies out of a morass of debt in the 1920s.

But economists and politicians need political ballast if they are to challenge the dominance of the finance sector. Such political ballast can be built by new progressive alliances – between that which we define broadly as industry and labor and the green movement. But first we need to provide solutions, and develop policies. The Green New Deal, and the proposals outlined above, is laid out here as a basis for discussion and debate, and in the hope that it can stimulate the formation of new, progressive alliances with which to challenge the dominance of finance over the economy. To return finance – in the words of the British Labour Party's 1944 manifesto – 'to its role as the servant, and the intelligent servant, of the community and productive industry; not their stupid master'.

The Green New Deal proposes the re-regulation of the finance sector – in particular the careful, system-wide regulation of the finance sector's powers to create credit. This will require introducing controls over the movement of capital – different from exchange controls – and restoring to publicly accountable central banks and governments the power to set interest rates.

To achieve this we must end the widespread use of the policy of 'inflation targeting' – a policy designed to suit the interests of bankers and the finance sector by maintaining high rates, and suppressing the price of wages.

Inflation targeting is what lies behind the collapse of the Hungarian economy. Hungarians, unable to afford the high rates of interest charged on mortgages in their own country, and encouraged by the central bank's policy of liberalizing capital flows, instead applied for mortgages in foreign currencies, most notably the Swiss franc. When high interest rates finally caused businesses and households in Hungary to buckle beneath the burden of their debts, the Hungarian currency, the forint, fell in value. This made the repayment of mortgages denominated in Swiss francs very expensive for Hungarian citizens.

High interest rates and the policy of inflation targeting are welcomed by creditors but are hard on debtors. There are far more debtors in the economy than savers. If we are to face both this financial crisis, and the threat of climate change, we need to abandon policies that lead to high rates of interest, and instead plan for *cheap, but not easy,* money to help finance investment in energy security.

Next, the US Federal Reserve, the European Central Bank, the Bank of England and other central banks should regain control over interest rates – all rates. Because the price of money is not determined by supply and demand – bank money is not a commodity but a costless, social construct – its price need never be high. The high rates set by the private sector are unacceptable in the midst of the worst global financial crisis in history. The interbank lending rate should no longer be set by a closed and non-transparent committee of private bankers. It must be set by a committee accountable to society, and, when setting rates, must consider the interests of *all* who make the economy work – labor and industry – not just finance.

To once again exercise control over all rates, the central banks will have to re-introduce capital controls. That might require a new international agreement, along the lines agreed at Bretton Woods in 1947.

Such changes are vital if we are to deal with this crisis. But they are vital too if we are to deal with two other major 'crunches'. The coming oil crunch, and the coming climate change crunch.

To create jobs it is vital that central banks build a framework of sustained, low rates of interest to enable affordable public and private investment in the Green New Deal's proposals. In particular, a massive public and private spending program is required to slash fossil fuel use and dramatically increase energy efficiency and use of renewables. This would open up a huge range of new business opportunities in places where people actually live, effectively raising a carbon army to fill countless green-collar jobs. This program, focusing initially on the goal of 'every building a power station', will involve traditional energy-saving measures such as insulation through to large-scale combined heat-and-power and a greatly accelerated uptake of renewable technology.

The Green New Deal will generate high skilled jobs in energy analysis, design and production of hi-tech renewable alternatives, and large-scale engineering projects such as combined heat and power and offshore wind. Lower skilled work will include loft lagging, draft stripping and fitting more efficient energy systems in homes, offices and factories.

In proposing such a strategy, we hope to correct a number of critical oversights. These include the ways in which environmentalists have tended to neglect the role of the finance sector and economic policy; how those involved in industry have generally failed to grasp the malign effects of the finance sector on the overall economy; and how trade unionists have for too long under-estimated the role of the finance sector and the threat of climate change.

We hope that the publication of the Green New Deal pamphlet by the New Economics Foundation will help bring these diverse social and industrial forces together, leading to a new progressive movement – an alliance between the labor movement and the green movement, between those engaged in manufacturing and the public sector, between civil society and academia, industry, agriculture and those working productively in the service industries.

Such a political alliance is vital if we are to challenge the dominance of the finance sector in the economy, its threat to the productive sectors of the economy, its corruption of the political system and its corrosion of social and environmental values.

All of this is do-able. Indeed urgently do-able. These are the system-wide fixes needed to deal with systemic threats – and the public expects the guardians of the nation's finances and security to implement them promptly.

Ann Pettifor is a fellow of the New Economics Foundation and co-author of *The Green New Deal* (www.neweconomics.org). In 2006 she authored the *The Coming First World Debt Crisis* (Palgrave 2006). She was a speaker at New Internationalist's *Clean Start* event in London on 15 December 2008. You can listen to her speech on www.newint.org/sites/cleanstart/video-ann-pettifor/

Connections: Susan George, p 49; Tarek El Diwany, p 85; Peter Stalker, p 97; John Christensen, p 115; Danny Chivers, p 193.

1 See Nouriel Roubini: 'Anatomy of a Financial Meltdown' http://tinyurl.com/27n22b See also Martin Wolf, 'America's economy risks the mother of all meltdowns', *The Financial Times*, 2 February 2008, http://tinyurl.com/cwh27p; and Prof Nouriel Roubini's blog on www.rgemonitor.com 2 FD Roosevelt, Inaugural speech, 1933.

NICOLA
...LLARD

RICHARD
WILKINSON &
KATE PICKETT

YASH
TANDON

BARBARA
EHRENREICH

JOHN
CHRISTENSEN

GEORGE
MONBIOT

S.

Not As It Seems

Noam Chomsky, interviewed by Sameer Dossani, discusses some of the less familiar facts behind the usual story of state capitalism in crisis.

SD In any first-year economics class, we are taught that markets have their ups and downs, so the current recession is perhaps nothing out of the ordinary. But this particular downturn is interesting for two reasons. First, market deregulation in the 1980s and 1990s made the boom periods artificially high, so the bust period will be deeper than it would otherwise have been. Second, despite an economy that's boomed since 1980, the majority of working-class US residents have seen their incomes stagnate. While the rich have done well, most of the country hasn't moved forward at all. Given the situation, my guess is that economic planners are likely to go back to some form of Keynesianism, perhaps not unlike the Bretton Woods system that was in place from 1948-71. What are your thoughts?

NC Well, I basically agree with your picture. In my view, the breakdown of the Bretton Woods system in the early 1970s is probably the major international event since 1945, much more significant in its implications than the collapse of the Soviet Union.

From roughly 1950 until the early 1970s there was a period of unprecedented and egalitarian economic growth. So the lowest quintile did as well – in fact they even did a little bit better – than the highest quintile. It was also a period of some limited but real benefits for the population. Social indicators, measurements of the health of society, very closely tracked growth. Many economists called it the golden age of modern capitalism – they should call it state capitalism, because government spending was a major engine of growth and development.

In the mid-1970s that changed. Bretton Woods restrictions on finance were dismantled, finance was freed, speculation boomed, huge amounts of capital started going into speculation against currencies and other paper manipulations, and the entire economy became financialized. The power of the economy shifted to the financial institutions, away from manufacturing.

Since then, the majority of the population has had a very tough time; in fact, it may be a unique period in American history. There's no other period where real wages – adjusted for inflation – have more or less stagnated for so long for a majority of the population and where living standards have stagnated or declined.

If you look at social indicators, they track growth pretty closely until 1975, and at that point they started to decline; so much so that now we're pretty much back to the level of 1960. There was growth, but it was highly inegalitarian – it went into a very small number of pockets. There have been brief periods in which this shifted. During the tech bubble in the late Clinton years, wages improved and unemployment went down. But these are slight deviations in a steady tendency of stagnation and decline for the majority of the population.

Financial crises have increased during this period, as predicted by a number of international economists. Once financial markets were freed up, there was expected to be an increase in financial crises, and that's happened. This crisis happens to be exploding in the rich countries, so people are talking about it, but it's been happening regularly around the world – some of them very serious – and not only are they increasing in frequency, they're getting deeper.

So the depth of the crisis is pretty severe – we're not at the bottom yet – and the architects of this are the people who are now designing Obama's economic policies. Dean Baker, one of the few economists who saw what was coming all along, pointed out that it's almost like appointing Osama bin Laden to run the so-called war on terror. Robert Rubin and Lawrence Summers, Clinton's Treasury Secretaries, are among the main architects of the crisis. Summers intervened strongly to prevent any regulation of derivatives and other exotic instruments. Rubin, who preceded him, was right in the lead of undermining the Glass-Steagall Act, all of which is pretty ironic. The Glass-Steagall Act protected commercial banks from risky investment firms, insurance firms, and so on, which kind of protected the core of the economy. That was broken up in 1999 largely under Rubin's influence. He immediately left the Treasury Department and became a director of Citigroup, which benefited from the breakdown of Glass-Steagall by expanding and becoming a 'financial supermarket', as they called it. Just to increase the irony (or the tragedy, if you like) Citigroup is now getting huge taxpayer subsidies. It's going back to trying to protect its commercial banking from risky side investments. Rubin resigned in disgrace – he's largely responsible for this. But he's one of Obama's major economic advisors. Summers is another one. Summer's protégé, Tim Geithner, is the Treasury Secretary.

People talk about a return to Keynesianism, but that's because of a systematic refusal to pay attention to the way the economy works. There's a lot of wailing now about 'socializing' the economy by bailing out financial institutions. Yeah, in a way we are, but that's icing on the cake. The whole economy's been socialized since – well actually forever, but certainly since the Second World War. This mythology, that the economy is based on entrepreneurial initiative and consumer choice – well, to an extent it is. For example, at the marketing end, you can choose one electronic device and not another. But the core of the economy relies very heavily on the state sector, and transparently so.

For example, take the last economic boom, which was based on information technology. Where did that come from? Computers and the internet. Computers and the internet were almost entirely within the state system for about 30 years – research, development, procurement, other devices – before they were finally handed over to private enterprise for profit-making.

The state sector is innovative and dynamic. It's true across the board, from electronics to pharmaceuticals to the new biology-based industries. The idea is that the public is supposed to pay the costs and take the risks. Ultimately, if there is any profit you hand it over to private tyrannies – corporations.

If you had to encapsulate the economy in one sentence, that would be the main theme. When you look at the details, of course it's a more complex picture. But that's the major theme. Socialization of risk and cost (but not profit) is partially new for the financial institutions – but it's just added on to what's been happening all along.

SD As we consider the picture of the collapse of some of these major financial institutions, we would do well to remember that some of these same policies have already been exported around the globe. Specifically, the International Monetary Fund (IMF) has forced an export-oriented growth model onto many countries, meaning that the current slowdown in US consumption is going to have major impacts in other countries. At the same time, some regions of the world, particularly the Southern Cone region of South America, are working to repudiate the IMF's market fundamentalist policies and build up alternatives. Can you talk a little about the international implications of the financial crisis? How is it that some of the institutions responsible for this mess, like the IMF, are using this as an opportunity to regain credibility on the world stage?

NC It's rather striking to notice that the consensus on how to deal with the crisis in the rich countries is almost the opposite of the consensus on how the poor countries should deal with similar economic crises. So when so-called developing countries have a financial crisis, the IMF rules are: raise interest rates, cut down economic growth, tighten the belt, pay off your debts (to us), privatize, and so on. That's the opposite of what's prescribed here. What's prescribed here is lower interest rates, pour government money into stimulating the economy, nationalize (but don't use the word), and so on. So yes, there's one set of rules for the weak and a different set of rules for the powerful. There's nothing novel about that.

As for the IMF, it is not an independent institution. It's pretty much a branch of the US Treasury Department – not officially, but that's pretty much the way it functions. The IMF was accurately described by a US Executive Director as 'the credit community's enforcer'. If a loan or an investment from a rich country to a poor country goes bad, the IMF makes sure that the lenders will not suffer.

If you had a capitalist system it wouldn't work like that. For example, suppose I lend you money, and I know that you may not be able to pay it back. I impose very high interest rates, so that at least I'll get that in case you crash. Then suppose at some point you can't pay the debt. Well, in a capitalist system it would be my problem. I made a risky loan, I made a lot of money from it by high interest rates and now you can't pay it back. OK, tough for me. That's a capitalist system.

But that's not the way our system works. If investors make

risky loans to, say, Argentina, get high interest rates and then Argentina can't pay it back, well that's when the IMF, the credit community's enforcer, steps in and says that the people of Argentina, they have to pay it back. Now, if you can't pay back a loan to me, I don't say that your neighbors have to pay it back. But that's what the IMF says. The IMF says the people of the country have to pay back the debt which they had nothing to do with – it was usually given to dictators, or rich élites, who sent it off to Switzerland or some place. But you guys, the poor folks living in the country, you have to pay it back.

Furthermore, if I lend money to you and you can't pay it back, in a capitalist system I can't ask my neighbors to pay me. But the IMF does – namely, the US taxpayer. They help make sure that the lenders and investors are protected. So yes, it's the credit community's enforcer. It's a radical attack on basic capitalist principles, just as the whole functioning of the economy based on the state sector is. But that doesn't change the rhetoric. It's kind of hidden in the woodwork.

What you said about the Southern Cone is exactly right. For the last several years they've been trying to extricate themselves from this whole neoliberal disaster. One of the ways was, for example, Argentina simply didn't pay back its debts, or rather restructured them and bought some of it back. Folks like the President of Argentina said that 'we're going to rid ourselves of the IMF' through these measures.

The IMF was in trouble. It was losing capital and losing borrowers, and therefore losing its ability to function as the credit community's enforcer. But this crisis is being used to restructure it and revitalize it.

It's also true that countries are driven to commodity-export; that's the mode of development that's designed for them. Then they will be in trouble if commodity prices fall. It's not 100-percent the case, but in the Southern Cone the countries that have been doing reasonably well do rely very heavily on commodity export, raw material export.

That's even true of the most successful of them, Chile, which is considered the darling. The Chilean economy has been based very heavily on copper exports. The biggest copper company in the world is CODELCO, the nationalized copper company – nationalized by President Salvador Allende – and nobody has tried to privatize it fully since, because it's such a cash cow. It has been undermined, so it controls less of copper exports than it has in the past, but it still provides a large part of the tax base of the Chilean economy and is also a large income producer. It's an efficiently run nationalized copper company. But reliance on copper export means you're vulnerable to a decline in the price of commodities. The other Chilean exports like, say, fruit and vegetables – which are adapted to the US market because of the seasonal differences – they're also vulnerable. And they haven't really done much in developing the economy beyond reliance on raw materials exports – a little, but not much.

The same can be said for the other currently successful countries. You look at growth rates in Peru and Brazil, they're heavily dependent on soy and other agricultural exports, or minerals; it's not a solid base for an economy.

One major exception to this is South Korea and Taiwan. They were very poor countries. South Korea in the late 1950s was probably about the level of Ghana today. But they developed by following the Japanese model – violating all the rules of the IMF and Western economists and developing pretty much the way the Western countries had developed, by substantial direction and involvement of the state sector.

So South Korea, for example, built a major steel industry, one of the most efficient in the world, by flatly violating the advice of the IMF and the World Bank, who said it was impossible. But they did it through state intervention, directing of resources, and also by restricting capital flight. Capital flight is a major problem for a developing country, and also for democracy. Capital flight could be controlled under Bretton Woods rules, but it was opened up in the last 30 years. In South Korea, you could get the death penalty for capital flight. So yes, they developed a pretty solid economy, as did Taiwan. China is a separate story, but they also radically violated the rules.

SD Do you think the current crisis will offer other countries the opportunity to follow the example of South Korea and Taiwan?

NC Well, you could say the example of the United States. During its major period of growth – late 19th century and early 20th century – the United States was probably the most protectionist country in the world. We had very high protective barriers, and it drew in investment. But private investment played only a supporting role. Take the steel industry. Andrew Carnegie built the first billion-dollar corporation by feeding off the state sector, building naval vessels and so on. This is Carnegie the great pacifist.

The sharpest period of economic growth in US history was during the Second World War, which was basically a semi-command economy, and industrial production more than tripled. That model pulled us out of the Depression, after which we became far and away the major economy in the world. After the Second World War, the substantial period of economic growth which I mentioned (1948-71) was very largely based on the dynamic state sector, and that remains true.

Let's take my own institution, MIT. I've been here since the 1950s, and you can see it first hand. In the 1950s and 1960s, MIT was largely financed by the Pentagon. There were labs that did classified war work, but the campus itself wasn't doing war work. It was developing the basis of the modern electronic economy: computers, the internet, microelectronics and so on. It was all developed under a Pentagon cover. IBM was here, learning how to shift from punch-cards to electronic computers.

It did get to a point by the 1960s that IBM was able to produce its own computers, but they were so expensive nobody could buy them, so the Government bought them.

In fact, procurement is a major form of government intervention in the economy, to develop the fundamental structure that will ultimately lead to profit. From the 1970s until today, the funding of MIT has been shifting away from the Pentagon and toward the National Institute of Health and related government institutions. Why? Because the cutting edge of the economy is shifting from an electronics base to a biology base. So now the public has to pay the costs of the next phase of the economy through other state institutions. Now, again, this is not the whole story, but it's a substantial part.

There will be a shift towards more regulation because of the current catastrophe. How long they can maintain paying off banks and financial institutions is not very clear. There will be more infrastructure spending, surely, because no matter where you are in the economic spectrum you realize that it's absolutely necessary. There will have to be some adjustment in the trade deficit, which is dramatic, meaning less consumption here, more export, and less borrowing.

And there's going to have to be some way to deal with the elephant in the closet, one of the major threats to the American economy, the increase in healthcare costs. Medicare is huge, and its costs are going way up. That's primarily because of the privatized healthcare system, which is highly inefficient. The US has twice the per capita costs of other industrialized countries, and it has some of the worst outcomes. The major difference between the US system and others is that this one is so heavily privatized, leading to huge administrative costs, bureaucratization, surveillance costs and so on. Now that's going to have to be dealt with somehow, because it's a growing burden on the economy and it's huge; it'll dwarf the federal budget if current tendencies persist.

SD Will the current crisis open up space for other countries to follow more meaningful development goals?

NC Well, it's been happening. One of the most exciting areas of the world is South America. For the last 10 years there have been quite interesting and significant moves towards independence, for the first time since the Spanish and Portuguese conquests. That includes steps towards unification, which is crucially important, and also beginning to address their huge internal problems. There's a new Bank of the South, based in Caracas, which hasn't really taken off yet, but it has prospects and is supported by other countries as well. MERCOSUR is a trading zone of the Southern Cone. Just recently, a new integrated organization has developed, UNASUR, the Union of South American Republics, and it's already been effective.

So when the US and the traditional ruling élites in Bolivia started moving towards a kind of secessionist movement, to try to undermine the democratic revolution that's taken place there, and when it turned violent, as it did, there was a meeting of UNASUR in September 2008 in Santiago. It issued a strong statement defending the elected president, Evo Morales, and condemning the violence and the efforts to undermine the democratic system. Morales responded by thanking them for their support and also saying that this is the first time in 500 years that South America's beginning to take its fate into its own hands.

That's significant; so significant that I don't even think it was reported [in the US]. Just how far these developments can go, both dealing with the internal problems and also the problems of unification and integration, we don't know, but the developments are taking place. There are also South-South relations developing, for example between Brazil and South Africa. This again breaks the imperial monopoly, the monopoly of US and Western domination.

China's a new element on the scene. Trade and investment are increasing, and this gives more options and possibilities to South America. The current financial crisis might offer opportunities for increasing this, but also it might go the other way. The financial crisis is of course harming – it must harm – the poor in the weaker countries and it may reduce their options.

These are really matters which will depend on whether popular movements can take control of their own fate, to borrow Morales' phrase. If they can, yes, there are opportunities.

Noam Chomsky, a founder of modern linguistic theory, is professor emeritus at the Massachusetts Institute of Technology. The author of many books critical of US foreign policy, he is an activist and associated with a wide range of radical causes.

Sameer Dossani, a *Foreign Policy In Focus* contributor, blogs at shirinandsameer.blogspot.com

This is an edited extract of an interview that first appeared on *Foreign Policy in Focus* www.fpif.org Reprinted with permission.

Connections: David Ransom p 11; Walden Bello, p 57; Barbara Ehrenreich, p 127; Evo Morales, p 165; John Hilary, p 217.

EVO
MORALES

NICOLA
BULLARD

RICHARD
WILKINSON &
KATE PICKETT

YASH
TANDON

BARBARA
EHRENREICH

JOHN
CHRISTENSEN

M.

Public Revolt Builds Against Rip-off Rescue Plans

The world is finally having its *¡Que se vayan todos!* moment, writes **Naomi Klein**.

Watching crowds in Iceland banging pots and pans until their government fell reminded me of a chant popular in anti-capitalist circles back in 2002: 'You are Enron. We are Argentina.'

Its message was simple enough. You – politicians and CEOs huddled at some trade summit – are like the reckless scamming execs at Enron (of course, we didn't know the half of it). We – the rabble outside – are like the people of Argentina, who, in the midst of an economic crisis eerily similar to our own, took to the street banging pots and pans. They shouted: *¡Que se vayan todos!* ('All of them must go!') and forced out a procession of four presidents in less than three weeks. What made Argentina's 2001-02 uprising unique was that it wasn't directed at a particular political party or even at corruption in the abstract. The target was the dominant economic model – this was the first national revolt against contemporary deregulated capitalism.

It's taken a while, but from Iceland to Latvia, South Korea to Greece, the rest of the world is finally having its *¡Que se vayan todos!* moment.

The stoic Icelandic matriarchs beating their pots flat even as their kids ransack the fridge for projectiles (eggs, sure, but *yogurt?*) echo the tactics made famous in Buenos Aires. So does the collective rage at élites who trashed a once thriving country and thought they could get away with it. As Gudrun Jonsdottir, a 36-year-old Icelandic office worker, put it: 'I've just had enough of this whole thing. I don't trust the government, I don't trust the banks, I don't trust the political parties and I don't trust the IMF. We had a good country, and they ruined it.'

Another echo: in Reykjavik, the protesters clearly wouldn't be bought off by a mere change of face at the top (even if the new PM *was* a lesbian). They wanted aid for people, not just banks; criminal investigations into the debacle; and deep electoral reform.

Similar demands could be heard in Latvia, whose economy contracted more sharply than any country in the EU, and where the government teetered on the brink. For weeks the capital was rocked by protests, including a full-blown, cobblestone-hurling riot on 13 January 2009. As in Iceland, Latvians were appalled by their leaders' refusal to take any responsibility for the mess. Asked by Bloomberg TV what caused the crisis, Latvia's finance minister shrugged: 'Nothing special.'

But Latvia's troubles are indeed special: the very policies that allowed the 'Baltic Tiger' to grow at a rate of 12 per cent in 2006 also caused it to contract violently: money, freed of all barriers, flowed out as quickly as it flowed in, with plenty being diverted to political pockets. (It is no coincidence that many of today's basket cases are yesterday's 'miracles': Ireland, Estonia, Iceland, Latvia.)

Something else Argentina-esque is in the air. In 2001 Argentina's leaders responded to the crisis with a brutal International Monetary Fund-prescribed austerity package: $9 billion in spending cuts, much of it hitting health and education. This proved to be a fatal mistake. Unions staged a general strike, teachers moved their classes to the streets and the protests never stopped.

This same bottom-up refusal to bear the brunt of the crisis unites many protests now. In Latvia, much of the popular rage focused on government austerity measures – mass lay-offs, reduced social services and slashed public sector salaries, all to qualify for an IMF emergency loan (no, nothing has changed). In Greece, December 2008's riots followed a police shooting of a 15-year-old. But what kept them going, with farmers taking the lead from students, was widespread rage at the government's crisis response: banks got a $36-billion bailout while workers got their pensions cut and farmers received next to nothing. Despite the inconvenience caused by tractors blocking roads, 78 per cent of Greeks said the farmers' demands were reasonable. Similarly, in France a general strike – triggered in part by President Sarkozy's plans to reduce the number of teachers dramatically – inspired the support of 70 per cent of the population.

Perhaps the sturdiest thread connecting this global backlash is a rejection of the logic of 'extraordinary politics' – the phrase coined by Polish politician Leszek Balcerowicz to describe how, in a crisis, politicians can ignore legislative rules and rush through unpopular 'reforms'. That trick is getting tired, as South Korea's government recently discovered. In December 2008, the ruling party tried to use the crisis to ram through a highly controversial free trade agreement with the United States. Taking closed-door politics to new extremes, legislators locked themselves in the chamber so they could vote in private, barricading the door with desks, chairs and couches.

Opposition politicians were having none of it: with sledgehammers and an electric saw, they broke in and staged a 12-day sit-in of Parliament. The vote was delayed, allowing for more debate – a victory for a new kind of 'extraordinary politics'.

Here in Canada, politics is markedly less YouTube-friendly –

but it has still been surprisingly eventful. In October 2008 the Conservative Party won national elections on an unambitious platform. Six weeks later, our Tory prime minister found his inner ideologue, presenting a budget bill that stripped public sector workers of the right to strike, canceled public funding for political parties and contained no economic stimulus. Opposition parties responded by forming a historic coalition that was only prevented from taking power by an abrupt suspension of Parliament. The Tories have come back with a revised budget: the pet right-wing policies have disappeared, and it is packed with economic stimulus.

The pattern is clear: governments that respond to a crisis created by free-market ideology with an acceleration of that same discredited agenda will not survive to tell the tale. As Italy's students have taken to shouting in the streets: 'We won't pay for your crisis!'

Naomi Klein is an author and activist. Her latest book is *The Shock Doctrine: the rise of disaster capitalism*, Metropolitan Books, New York, 2008.

This article was first published in *The Nation* and is reprinted here with permission.

© Naomi Klein

Connections: David Ransom, p 11; Vanessa Baird, p 65; Barbara Ehrenreich, p 127.

GEORGE
MONBIOT
PETER
STALKER
TAREK EL
DIWANY
VANESSA
BAIRD
WALDEN
BELLO
SUSAN
GEORGE

No More
of the Same

Susan George thinks there is plenty of scope for what she calls 'Green Keynesianism'. She was in conversation with Adam Ma'anit.

AM Are you in favor of regulating the banks?

SG Everyone now agrees on control and regulation – it would be difficult not to, considering the crisis we're now in. Regulation should not be the major problem, but who does it and how should be of interest to progressive people, because that will be the debate. At present, despite a few efforts of the Bank for International Settlements, all regulation stops at national borders. We need international regulation and international taxation, the abolition of tax havens and taxes across borders, particularly of financial transactions and currency speculation.

I joked on French television recently that we're expecting Prime Minister François Fillon and President Nicolas Sarkozy to sign up with ATTAC at any time, because they are both now in favor of getting rid of tax havens. Fillon calls them 'black holes'. That shows that you can change a lot of minds very quickly if the system gets a big enough shock.

It would be to the advantage of governments to close tax havens because that alone would generate at least an extra $250 billion for governments to play with. They couldn't always say 'We don't have enough money to do this or that. We can't provide social safety nets or improve education and the health system.' They would have no excuses.

Presently, transnational corporations pay very low or no taxes because they make use of the great differences in taxes in different jurisdictions. They should have to declare their sales, their costs, including salaries, and the taxes paid in each national jurisdiction, so that it would be easy to see what they pay where. This is known as a 'Unitary Profits Tax'. Corporations couldn't decide, for instance, to pay half their taxes in a very low tax jurisdiction where they make only a tiny percentage of their sales.

The banks must also contribute. The huge bank bailouts are disgraceful because one can find billions for the banks in half an hour, but citizens get nothing in return. Banks should be nationalized – I prefer the word 'socialized' because they should be under citizen control and then loan on a priority basis to ecological projects and to the South.

People are angry about the bailouts and the abuses by banks and their executives. Enough is enough. We should also call for total cancellation of 'Third World' debt, but under certain conditions. In exchange, Southern governments must also contribute to ecological transformation – through reforestation and the protection of their own ecosystems, biodiversity and soils.

Closing tax havens would contribute to development in the South as well. A recent study showed that between 1970 and 2004, $420 billion left Sub-Saharan Africa for private accounts. Much of that came from loans, with 60 per cent of those loans leaving the country the same year the loans were made. With interest added, that comes to more than $600 billion stolen from Africa, even though the loans stayed on the national books and poor people are paying them back with their sacrifices.

The élites that stole the funds should be named and shamed. The money should be sent back, carefully audited and used for productive causes.

I have never advocated that debt be canceled unconditionally. Ideally, each country should have to hold free, fair and observed elections to appoint both geographical and sectoral representatives to a supervisory council so that all sectors, including farmers, women, entrepreneurs, workers, even the army, everybody is represented. They should decide, alongside the government, how the money should be used that is no longer going for debt service. The council should decide the changes made to the national budgets.

My idea of conditionality is quite different from that of the IMF – I don't think outsiders should be making the decisions but, rather, the people of the countries concerned. There would still have to be specific conditions on ecological debt, for example obligatory reforestation, and many people on the Left disagree with me. But I don't trust the leadership except in a few countries, like Tanzania.

AM Would the nationalization and/or renationalization of banks offer any opportunities for change?

SG Definitely, but only when under citizen control. Banks would have to invest in good projects, particularly ecological ones. It would allow us to renegotiate the mortgages of people presently at risk of losing their homes, instead of foreclosing on them as has happened to millions in the US. Think of the ways President Roosevelt targeted government spending during the Depression.

AM But are governments really willing to do that? Is there sufficient political will for such active reshaping of the economy?

SG President Obama plans to target government investments and says he will invest in a Green New Deal, which is great. But in my view he is giving far too much to the banks, which given the shape they're in seems like pouring water into the sand. Gordon Brown seems to have decided to invest partly in aircraft carriers and new systems of nuclear dissuasion, which aside from a few jobs created will be totally unproductive.

I hope this crisis will change politics everywhere. People could, if they get organized, have more of a voice. Everything is in flux now and it's hard to say. Obviously, today we don't have the right governments. But a few months ago Sarkozy and Fillon were not saying 'close down tax havens' either.

AM Are they just being rhetorical, or are they backing those statements up with policy?

SG I think they mean it. They recognize they have a lot to lose. And the French, even on the Right, are more state-oriented than many other people – certainly more so than the British. They would probably like to seize the opportunity, it would be politically popular, because people are furious – but no single government has the power to make that kind of international decision. Don't forget that although everyone loves to hate the banks, the Brits control a great many tax havens like Jersey, Bermuda, the Virgin Islands and so on.

AM What strategies should we be using in order to try to win some political ground?

SG Denunciation is certainly not enough. We need to articulate a positive vision of what we can do in the face of this crisis to make some meaningful reforms. We have to seize this opportunity to control the banks and push for international taxation. Everything stops at national borders, yet we're living in a globalized world. That has implications for regulation, for investment and for citizen control.

Change takes time. Now everyone has to recognize that we – people in ATTAC and other NGOs, like me – were right and the others were wrong. They didn't foresee the crisis and we did. Some of our ideas seem perfectly normal to activists but quite new to the mainstream, and it's important to keep repeating the message because there is an opportunity for a shift. We must try to influence public opinion, the political parties and governments, meaning we must become mainstream ourselves, at least with some of our proposals. These people have failed. Everybody can see that now and they understand that unless governments do something very, very different, they too will fail. That's why profound change is a win-win strategy.

AM Would you define your concrete proposals as 'Ecological Keynesianism'?

SG That's what I've been doing! A Green New Deal is rational, affordable and deliverable. We already have most of the knowledge, technology and skills we need. Some green technologies are expensive now but once they are mass produced, the costs go down immediately.

AM What about the International Monetary Fund (IMF) and the World Bank?

SG The World Bank has spent its entire career financing terrible projects. It just got another $6 billion at the last G7 to be the 'ecological bank' whereas it has been spending billions right up to this day on fossil fuel and coal-mining projects. Nobody deserves ecological funds less than the Bank. They may, at best, invest in slightly less awful technology than the worst technology available.

The IMF has got a huge shot in the arm with the G20 that tripled its resources. If it makes loans using the same Washington Consensus conditions as before, we're done for. I hope that people campaigning against the Bank and the Fund will be able to make it clear that these are totally undemocratic institutions. They listen only to the most powerful member governments.

AM But Keynes had a dream about them as well...

SG Indeed he did. Part of it came true but most didn't, especially when neoliberalism took over completely towards the end of the 1970s and became the only doctrine of the Bank and the Fund. Keynes also wanted a trade organization with a financing arm and a currency called the bancor which would have prevented the huge deficits and huge surpluses we see today in countries like the US and China. His system guaranteed that if you had too big a surplus you would have to revalue your currency, making your goods more expensive. If you had too big a deficit, you would have to devalue, so your goods would become more attractive and you could sell more of them. If you didn't, you would have to pay taxes both on deficits and on surpluses into a central fund. The larger the deficit or surplus, the higher the tax, so governments would react quickly. We could take out the Havana Charter, dust it off and adapt it. It might not have prevented the financial crisis, but it would have been better than the WTO, and probably would have prevented the rise of tax havens as well. Keynes' vision even had provisions for the protection of nature – incredibly enough, in the 1940s – and for working people, as well as guarantees about commodity prices.

AM What are the biggest threats we face now?

SG The biggest threat is more of the same. If we don't act now, the biggest danger is global warming which will multiply hugely all our problems. If governments don't take this crisis seriously, if they don't use the financial crisis to check global warming, we're in for a seriously bad time.

Susan George is president of the Board of the Transnational Institute in Amsterdam, and honorary president of ATTAC (Association for Taxation of Financial Transactions to Aid Citizens). She is the author of 14 books written in French and English and widely translated. Her most recent books are *Hijacking America: How the Religious and Secular Right Changed What Americans Think* (Polity Press 2008) and *We the Peoples of Europe* (Pluto Press 2008).

Adam Ma'anit is a former co-editor of *New Internationalist* magazine.

Connections: Ann Pettifor, p 21; Walden Bello, p 57; Peter Stalker, p 97; John Christensen, p 115; John Hilary, p 217.

DEREK WALL
MICHAEL ALBERT
EVO MORALES
NICOLA BULLARD
RICHARD WILKINSON & KATE PICKETT
YASH TANDON
EHR

Goodbye Washington Consensus, Hello Global Social Democracy?

Like generals, argues Walden Bello, the democratic left may still be fighting the last war – against neoliberalism, which is already dead. The new contest is with a global version of what the 'New Deal' did for national economies in the 1930s; and now, as then, ideas alone are not enough.

There is real panic out there within the establishment, real disarray: a sinking feeling that things will get worse before they get better. Increasingly, the more intelligent intellectuals of the establishment are realizing that we are just at the beginning of the global freefall and don't really know when we are going to hit rock bottom – or, once we reach it, how long the global economy will lie there.

Indeed, the best image one can conjure up of the global economy is that of a German World War Two submarine that has been depth-charged in the mid-Atlantic. It's descending rapidly to the ocean bottom. Will the crew get some compressed air into the badly damaged ballast tanks and get back to the surface, as in Wolfgang Petersen's classic film *Das Boot?* Or will the U-boat just stay at the bottom?

Will Keynesian methods of economic reflation work today? The more critical establishment thinkers, like Martin Wolf of the *Financial Times* and Nobel laureate Paul Krugman, are not taking bets on it.

57

Two things one can be certain of: one, neoliberal approaches are thoroughly discredited; two, the facts on the ground will dictate what those who wish to save the system will do. So let us disabuse ourselves of the notion that neoliberal principles will constitute red lines beyond which they will not go.

Let us be more specific. The actions of the new Obama administration in Washington clearly constitute a break with neoliberalism. One important question, of course, is how decisive and definitive the break will be. Other questions, however, go to the heart of capitalism itself. Will government ownership, intervention and control be exercised simply to stabilize capitalism, after which control will be given back to the corporate élites? Are we going to see a second round of Keynesian capitalism, where the state works out a partnership with corporate and labor élites based on industrial policy, growth and high wages – though with a green dimension this time around? Or will we witness the beginnings of fundamental shifts in the ownership and control of the economy in a more popular direction? There are limits to the reform of global capitalism, but at no time in the last half-century have those limits seemed more fluid.

Massive stimulus spending at record-breaking levels – anathema to neoliberals – has become practice, the only difference among Northern élites being how much it will take to refloat the submarine. On this, Obama has become super-Keynesian. Nationalization of the banks – another practice condemned by neoliberalism – is also well under way. The questions that divide the élites are how aggressively the government will exercise its control of the majority shares of the stocks, and whether it will return the banks to private management once the crisis is over.

The task at hand for the state managers of capitalism is not whether solutions are in line with a discredited doctrine, but what it will take to save capitalism. Beyond deficit spending and nationalization, the debate is likely to be about whether to go along the path of what one can call, for want of a better term, 'Global Social Democracy', or GSD.

Even before the full unfolding of the financial crisis, partisans of GSD had already been positioning this as an alternative to neoliberal globalization. One person associated with it is British Prime Minister Gordon Brown, who led the initial European response to the financial meltdown via the partial nationalization of the banks. Brown, while he was still Chancellor, proposed what he called an 'alliance capitalism' between market and state institutions. It would reproduce on the global stage what Brown said Franklin Roosevelt had done for the national economy, by 'securing the benefits of the market while taming its excesses'. This must be a system, continued Brown, that 'captures the full benefits of global markets and capital flows, minimizes the risk of disruption, maximizes opportunity for all and lifts up the most vulnerable – in short, the restoration in the international economy of public purpose and high ideals'.[1]

Joining Brown in the discourse has been a diverse group including the economist Jeffrey Sachs, the financier George Soros, former UN Secretary-General Kofi Annan, the sociologist David Held, Nobel laureate Joseph Stiglitz, even Bill Gates. There are, of course, differences of nuance, but the thrust of their perspectives is the same: to bring about a reformed social order and a reinvigorated ideological consensus for global capitalism.

Among their key propositions are the following:

- Globalization is beneficial for the world; neoliberals have simply botched the job of managing it and selling it to the public.
- It is urgent to save globalization from the neoliberals because it is reversible and may, in fact, already be in the process of being reversed.
- Growth must not be accompanied by increasing inequality.
- Trade must be promoted but subjected to social and

environmental conditions.

- Unilateralism must be avoided, while at the same time preserving – by fundamentally reforming – multilateral institutions and agreements.
- Global social integration, or reduced inequalities both within and across countries, must accompany global market integration.
- The global debt of developing countries must be canceled or radically reduced, so the resulting savings can be used to stimulate the local economy, thus contributing to global reflation.
- Poverty and environmental degradation are so severe that a massive aid program or 'Marshall Plan' from the North to the South must be mounted, within the framework of the UN Millennium Development Goals.
- A 'Second Green Revolution' must be set in motion, especially in Africa, through the widespread adoption of genetically engineered seeds.
- Huge investments must be devoted to push the global economy along more environmentally sustainable paths, with government taking a leading role ('Green Keynesianism' or 'Green Capitalism').

GSD has not received much critical attention, perhaps because, like the French generals at the start of the Second World War, many progressives are still fighting the last war – that is, against neoliberalism. A critique is urgent, and not only because GSD is neoliberalism's most likely successor. More important, although it has some positive elements, it has a number of problematic features.

A critique might begin by highlighting problems with four central elements.

First, GSD shares neoliberalism's bias for globalization, but promises to promote it better than the neoliberals. Globalization here means the 'rapid integration of production and markets but with effective regulation', according to Gert-Jan Koopman at the European Commission, who describes himself as a Keynesian. This amounts to saying that simply by adding the dimension of regulation, along with 'global social integration', a socially and ecologically destructive process can be made palatable. It assumes that people really want to be part of an integrated global economy. But might they not in fact prefer to be part of economies that are subject to local control and buffered from the vagaries of the international economy? The recent swift downward trajectory of interconnected economies underscores one of the anti-globalization movement's key criticisms of the process.

Second, GSD shares neoliberalism's preference for the market, differentiating itself mainly by advocating state action to address market failures. The kind of globalization the world needs, according to Jeffrey Sachs in *The End of Poverty*, would entail 'harnessing... the remarkable power of trade and investment while acknowledging and addressing limitations through compensatory collective action'.[2] This is very different from saying that the citizenry and civil society must make the key economic decisions and that the market, like the state bureaucracy, is only one mechanism for democratic decision-making.

Third, GSD is a technocratic project, with experts hatching and pushing reforms on society from above, rather than a participatory project with initiatives percolating from the ground up. The aim of an alternative project must be to win more space for democratic decision-making away from the market – and from the technocracy.

Fourth, GSD, while critical of neoliberalism, accepts the framework of monopoly capitalism. This rests on the concentrated private control of the means of production. It derives profit from the exploitative extraction of surplus value from labor, is driven from crisis to crisis by tendencies toward overproduction, and pushes the environment to its limits. Like traditional Keynesianism in the national arena, GSD seeks in the global arena a new class compromise that is accompanied by new methods to contain capitalism's tendency toward crisis. Just as the old Social Democracy and the New Deal stabilized national capitalism, the historical function of Global Social Democracy is to iron out the contradictions of contemporary global capitalism and to re-legitimize it after the chaos left by neoliberalism.

The differences between Global Social Democracy and the democratic left are clear:

- GSD is about social management. The democratic left is about social liberation.
- GSD is about technocratic management. The democratic left is about participatory democracy.
- GSD is about reconfiguring monopoly capitalism. The democratic left is about creating a post-capitalist system.
- GSD is about perfecting globalization. The democratic left is about deglobalization.
- GSD sees the future in Green Capitalism. The democratic left sees replacing capitalism as a precondition for an ecologically benign social organization of the planet.

Like President Lula of Brazil, President Obama has a talent for the rhetorical bridging of different political discourses. He is also a 'blank slate' when it comes to economics. Like President Roosevelt, he is not bound to the formulas of the *ancien régime*. Like Lula and Roosevelt, he is a pragmatist whose key criterion is success at social management. As such, he is uniquely positioned to lead this ambitious reformist enterprise.

Our task will be not merely to support the positive aspects of the GSD program that promote social and environmental welfare, while opposing those that lead to monopoly capitalism; more important, it will be to differentiate our own enterprise and win people over to our strategic vision and program.

However, the choice in the coming period is not going to boil down to one between the democratic left and global social democracy. Would that it were that simple! In fact, there could be a response that is anti-neoliberal in its economic rhetoric and populist in its social policy, but exclusionist in its politics, evoking tribal as opposed to people's solidarity.

We can already see something of this in the approach of President Nicolas Sarkozy in France. Declaring that 'laissez-faire capitalism is dead', he has created a strategic investment fund of $20 billion to promote technological innovation, keep advanced industries in French hands and save jobs. 'The day we don't build trains, airplanes, automobiles and ships, what will be left of the French economy?' he asked. 'Memories. I will not make France a simple tourist reserve.'[3]

This kind of aggressive industrial policy, aimed at shoring up key sectors of the French capitalist class and winning over the country's traditional white working class, can go hand-in-hand with the exclusionary anti-immigrant policies with which the French President has been associated.

Sarkozy's conservative populism is relatively mild. There are more radical ones waiting in the wings, like the anti-Muslim movement of Gerd Wilders in the Netherlands, with the same mix of communal solidarity, populist economics and authoritarian leadership. There are such movements everywhere in the developed and developing world, and one urgent concern is that in the crisis they might make their breakthrough.

The point is that things will become worse, much worse, before they become better. The global crisis is not something that can be managed to a soft landing, like the US Airways flight that was eased on to the Hudson River in New York. If global social democracy fails in its effort to reinvigorate capitalism, and the democratic left is unable to come out with a vision that appeals to people, then other forces will step in to fill the vacuum, as they did in the 1930s. If there is anything that the vast literature on fascism can teach us today, it is that good will, values and vision are not enough. In the end, politics – an effective strategy of coalition-building and wise, supple tactics – is decisive.

To conclude, while progressives were engaged in full-scale war against neoliberalism, reformist thinking was already percolating into critical establishment circles. This thinking is now becoming policy, and progressives must work double time to engage it. It is not just a matter of moving from criticism to prescription. The challenge is to overcome the limits to the progressive political imagination imposed by the neoliberal challenge in the 1980s, combined with the collapse of the bureaucratic socialist regimes in the early 1990s.

Progressives should aspire once again to equality and participatory democratic control of both the national and the global economy. Ideas are not enough. Politics must once more be in command.

Walden Bello is President of the Freedom from Debt Coalition, Senior Analyst at Focus on the Global South, and Professor of Sociology at the University of the Philippines.

1 Gordon Brown, 'Government and supranational agencies: a New Consensus', in John Dunning, ed, *Making Globalization Good*, Oxford University Press, 2003. 2 Jeffrey Sachs, *The End of Poverty*, Penguin, New York, 2005. 3 Elitsa Vucheva, 'Sarkozy Launches €20 Billion "Strategic" Industries Fund', *EUObserver.com*, http://euobserver.com/9/27157.

The original version of this essay appeared originally on *Foreign Policy in Focus* www.fpif.org but has been substantially revised for this book by Walden Bello.

Connections: David Ransom, p 11; Noam Chomsky, p 33; Susan George, p 49; Yash Tandon p 131; John Hilary, p 217.

Naked Emperors

Vanessa Baird gets basic – and personal.

We should thank Bernard Madoff – the Wall Street broker with 'impeccable credentials' who swindled investors (including some of his best friends) to the tune of $50 billion. Few individuals have so eloquently exposed how easily gulled are the supposed experts of the financial world.

Madoff highlighted a simple truth: that one of the best ways to fool people is to make things appear rather complicated. Vanity kept 'sophisticated investors' from admitting that they didn't really understand how Madoff's get-richer-even-quicker scheme actually worked. Greed and laziness kept them from asking the crucial questions. As long as the money came rolling in – and at 15 per cent the returns were abnormally high – who cared?

There are lessons to be learned from this story – such as don't place too much faith in 'the experts' and don't be scared to ask simple questions, however naïve they may appear.

To be radical you need to get down to the roots of things. And in an era that has been dominated by those who trade in obfuscation, simplicity may be the best tool we've got for cutting through the bullshit.

1 What are BANKS for?

To link borrowers and savers. In theory, banks help to keep money flowing and offer some stability... Don't laugh.

What have they become?

Gambling dens. Major high-street banks, especially in the US and Britain, took advantage of deregulation to move into the high-profit, high-risk activity usually undertaken by speculators. Carried along by greed and free-market fever, they played the international markets using complex new financial 'instruments' they didn't understand, with little or no idea of whom they were lending to. By statute, banks are allowed to lend several times more than the amount deposited with them by savers. The illusion of safety is only maintained because they have the backing of the state. However, the more aggressive players (like Northern Rock in Britain) took it to dizzying extremes, lending more and more multiples of their deposits. The frenzy encouraged debt, fed consumerism, and made fat profits for shareholders and top executives. Some retail banks (like RBS in Britain or Citicorp in the US) grew exponentially, buying up other banks, including investment banks. Buried under mountains of bad debt, ailing banks froze lending and became like menacing beggars. Too big to be allowed to fail, they have been bailed out by governments using... our money, in the form of taxes we shall have to pay in future.

Does it have to be that way?

No. Traditional building societies or mutual savings banks are still owned by their customers (rather than by their shareholders). Some have taken too many risks, but generally they are more restricted in the way they can raise funds and need to keep a more sustainable balance between their deposits and what they lend. Ethical banks, too, operate more cautiously than their non-ethical counterparts, avoiding risky speculation and international money markets. They are more responsive to human rights, the environment, and the communities they serve. In addition around 170 million people in 96 countries in the world today belong to credit unions – co-operatively run mutual associations or people's banks that are often established in areas where people find it hard to get credit.

What could be done?
Even bankers' organizations have been forced to admit that their sector needs more robust regulation. Radical reform is possible. All speculative activity known to cause instability could be banned outright; other forms could be taxed. Banks could be forced to become transparent and publicly accountable. Running a bank, which is a public utility, is a privilege; its abuse could be punished severely. There would be an end to bank bailouts that spread the risk to the public while the profits remain private – outright nationalization is preferable since 'private enterprise knows best' quite clearly no longer applies. The duty of banks is to lend in ways that meet people's social and economic needs. If bankers think this is incompatible with commercial banking they should look at the highly successful Grameen Bank in Bangladesh which extends micro-credit to people (especially women) considered too poor to be 'credit worthy'. Grameen customers' rate of repayment is exemplary. Similarly, credit unions lend to those who need it most. These existing popular forms of banking could be strengthened, new ones encouraged. The size of banks could be restricted so that none is allowed to get 'too big to fail'. The division between commercial and investment banks could be reinstated. Finally, there needs to be binding regulation of the banking system at an international level.

What can I do?

How about putting your custom with a popular banking organization such as a credit union, mutual savings institution or building society? If you need to use a commercial bank, go for an ethical one. Recognize that the two statements: 'Your money is safe with us' and 'we will earn you high returns' are contradictory. Consider non-interest systems – such as genuine Islamic lending, whereby profits and losses are shared by lender and borrower. Add your voice to campaigns for tight regulation of banks and more ethical, accountable and sustainable banking. Banks exist to serve the public – not the other way round. The banks belong to us – and in the case of recently bailed-out ones (RBS, Northern Rock, HBOS, Merrill Lynch, Fanny Mae, Freddy Mac) quite literally so!

You may want to check out *www.banktrack.org* – an international coalition of civil society individuals and organizations that examines what banks do.

2 What are HOUSES for?

Living in. Making 'home'.

What have they become?

Property. Investment opportunities. During the boom, getting on to the property ladder was seen as a way of making more money than you could by working. Rising prices made houses too expensive to buy, but irresponsible lending filled the gap. In 2008 high-risk or 'sub-prime' mortgages triggered defaults and the imminent collapse of US banks. Shockwaves spread through the global economy as it became clear that the 'toxic' mortgages had been sold and resold in 'bundles' on the international markets.

Does it have to be that way?

Contrary to propaganda, being saddled with a mortgage is not the only route to happiness. Social housing and housing associations can provide decent homes for those who cannot afford to buy or for whom buying doesn't make sense – which, were it not for the dynamics of property speculation, would probably be most of us. Not all societies have seen property booms on the scale of Britain or the US. Germany, for example, has a large, decent-quality rental sector.

What could be done?

If governments embarked on major social housing projects, this would help tackle homelessness and provide employment. Expanding housing stocks would also guard against another property boom. Housing associations, co-ops and other community housing organizations could be encouraged, supported and given greater scope to provide homes. There should be a moratorium on evicting people who have fallen into arrears because of the crash. Mortgages should be rescheduled. Government loans or offers to buy properties would add them to the public housing stock, renting them back to current householders. Various forms of co-ownership could be developed. Housing could be made cheaper if houses and land were legally separated; the land would be communally owned while individuals could own or co-own houses.

What can I do?

Don't let politicians and bankers off the hook. Through a combination of deregulation and irresponsible lending they have exposed citizens to untold risk. Organize with others to create supportive networks to fight evictions, using direct action if necessary. Reassert the human right to shelter and the duty of the state to prioritize this. Support housing charities and homelessness campaign groups or street newspapers in your country. There are lessons to be learned from community groups in countries like India, South Africa and Brazil. You could check out the Centre for Housing Rights and Evictions (www.cohre. org). This is an NGO with offices around the world that exposes and fights forced evictions.

3 What are JOBS for?
To earn money for the essentials of life. A job may also bring personal satisfaction and be a means of contributing to society.

What have they become?
A means to deepen inequality. Globalization has helped keep wages low for millions around the world, increasing profit margins for corporations and shareholders. As top executive incomes soared, helped by generous bonuses, average employee salaries decreased in real terms. Today, jobs are a focus for fear and anxiety as recession bites and unemployment looms. Many business leaders are now pitting jobs against environmental obligations. It's an 'either/or' situation, they assert: tackling climate change will cost jobs.

Does it have to be that way?
No. Employment and environmentalism are not diametric opposites.

What could be done?
Tens of millions of 'green collar' jobs could be created in the coming years, according to the UN's International Labour Organization. Jobs could be created in renewable energy production, sustainable transport, eco-building and retrofitting, and organic food production. This could be the dawn of a new era of decent jobs in a sustainable low-carbon world. Eco-engineering, to develop cleaner technology and production methods, could be applied in traditional industries across the board. A policy of major public spending (or 'green Keynesianism') could boost economies.

As a condition of receiving public money, businesses would be bound to 'green' their activities: auto makers need to develop green, energy efficient models, for example, which, through subsidies or incentives, would be cheaper to the consumer than more polluting models. Low-cost finance capital should be available to genuinely green, co-operative or social enterprises. Using 'Just Transition' principles, workers in ailing industries could be retrained.

What can I do?

Act to save jobs and create new ones. If you don't belong to a union, join one now. Campaign within your own workplace against fat-cat salaries and bonuses; support calls for a maximum wage to reduce pay differentials. If the company you work for is going bust, organize with other workers to take over the company and run it yourselves, co-operatively. Seems far-fetched? It's what Argentinean workers at the Brukman textile factory in Buenos Aires did, saving their jobs and their company. Times of fear and uncertainty can encourage fascist tendencies, so be prepared to challenge racists who use the recession to scapegoat migrant workers. Anger might be more appropriately directed towards overpaid mis-managers. And finally: if money can be conjured up to save banks, it can be summoned up to save jobs.

4 What are MARKETS for?

Places where goods can be bought and sold.

What have they become?

God. As in 'the wisdom' or 'the hidden hand' of the Market. This belief underpins the dogma of free trade and privatization that has dominated the globe for the past 30 years. It has worked in favor of rich-world corporations and developing-world élites, while deepening inequality, poverty and indebtedness worldwide. World Trade Organization (WTO) provisions to liberalize financial services have created a dangerously integrated global system based on a bad model.

Does it have to be that way?

Most Western political and business leaders are still acting as though the 'one-size-fits-all' free trade model were the only show in town. Any alternative is condemned as 'economic nationalism' or 'protectionism' – repeatedly, and incorrectly, blamed for the 1930s Depression actually caused by catastrophic bank failure. International trade does not have to destroy local economies or the environment if it is conducted in a rational and flexible way. Local or regional trade agreements, between equals (such as ALBA in South America) may be fairer and more beneficial to those involved.

What could be done?

The World Trade Organization could acknowledge that the model it has been pushing through the current Doha round of negotiations is fundamentally flawed. The WTO needs to be scrapped for the sake of fairness, democracy and ecological responsibility. Perhaps the role of negotiating international trade should move to the United Nations. Within these negotiations, individual countries should be free to adopt policies that do not harm and impoverish their own people; developing nations, in particular, must be able to protect their local environments from the activities of transnational corporations. The judicious use of subsidies and tariffs (anathema to free-marketeers), should be available options in a toolbox of trade strategies.

What can I do?

The G20 (the self-appointed group of the world's biggest economies) is acting as though it speaks for the world and can shape the global economy. It does not speak for most of the world's people and needs to be loudly reminded of the fact whenever it meets. Determined to patch up the disastrous global free market, the G20 is turning a blind eye to alternatives being developed by civil society and global justice movements around the world. But we must carry on developing and presenting alternatives. Even at an individual consumer level you can support and keep sustaining the kind of markets and the type of trading you want to see more of.

5 What's MONEY for?
A handy medium for exchange or barter. It can be anything – rabbits' tails, shells, metal discs, even bits of paper – that people agree is 'money'.

What's it become?
Most money today is created not by governments but by banks – in Britain, for example, commercial banks create 95 per cent of the country's money. They do this by making loans. If one dollar is deposited with a bank by one person, the bank is allowed to lend one dollar to ten people on the back of that one dollar deposit. Another way of using money to make money is to speculate on exchange rates between different currencies. Thanks to computer technology this happens at breakneck speed and can cause extreme instability in international money markets. An attack on one currency – the Thai baht or the British pound, for example – can bring a country to its knees within hours. Some currencies are safer than others, though. The US's unilateral decision to leave the Gold Standard in 1971 made the dollar the global currency 'of last resort'. Major transactions are conducted in dollars – other countries, such as China or India, hold most of their sovereign wealth in dollars. Other currencies may be allowed to crash, but no-one can afford to let the dollar fail.

Does it have to be that way?
Not everyone believes so. Many people believe that the money

system has become too complicated, and far too tangled up with banks, debt and speculation.

What could be done?
Recent events have proved that the current system of allowing banks to create most of the money in the system is far too risky. If this function were to return to central banks, the system would become less profitable for private banks and more stable for the rest of us. At an international level, the dominance of one country's currency (the US dollar) needs to be challenged and a return to an equivalent of the former Gold Standard agreed. Taxing cross-border transactions, meanwhile, is an easy way to put the brakes on currency speculation.

What can I do?
There are numerous civil society groups around the world campaigning for more stable currencies. You might want to use local currencies alongside national ones. The Lewes Pound, for example, can be used in shops in this English town. You can bypass currency altogether by using the Local Exchange Trading System (LETS). This operates at a community level in several countries including the US, Britain, Australia and Canada. With LETS, goods and services are exchanged without money passing hands.

6 What's CREDIT for?

Individuals and companies need credit to buy what they need now and can pay for later. The word credit comes from the Latin 'to believe'...

What's it become?
Once frowned upon, in recent times buying things on the 'never-never' has become a way of life. Credit has been pushed like heroin, with little regard for the financial health – or credit-

worthiness – of the borrower. Banks and credit-card companies made money by getting people into debt. Retailers made money selling consumers things they couldn't afford. Governments were re-elected on the back of economic growth fueled by unsustainable credit booms and runaway consumption. During the 1980s, the extension of international credit led to debt crises in many countries of the Majority World. Poor countries were in hock to rich ones that pushed the dogma of economic liberalization onto the poor, using the International Monetary Fund and the World Bank as their 'enforcers'. Our global economic system is based on debt and only works if credit is constantly available and keeps flowing. But this only happens if there is faith in the system. If faith dries up, so does the system. Easy credit has become toxic debt. In recent times governments have tried to restore faith (or 'confidence') by throwing taxpayers' money at the problem in the form of 'fiscal stimulus' packages.

Does it have to be that way?

Countries where people have saved more and borrowed less are not so likely to be paralyzed by credit crunches. China has been sucked into the world recession, and its export-led economic model is certainly taking a hammering. But its high level of savings gives it more flexibility than credit-crunched Iceland, for example, which has had to go cap in hand to the IMF. Similarly, governments which have paid off their debts to the international financial institutions have more space for developing socially responsive economic policies.

What could be done?

Citizens in Europe, the Americas, India and Australia are footing massive bills for 'fiscal stimulus' packages to bolster their economies. These citizens have a right to insist on certain conditions. For example, the packages should a) meet the needs of the poorest and most vulnerable first, and b) meet environmental criteria for tackling climate change. Public money should not be not be used to line the pockets of executives and shareholders. Governments could encourage schemes to enable individuals to extend or renegotiate their loans and credit-card debts. On the international scene, irresponsible loans to poor countries should be canceled.

What can I do?

If you are strapped for cash, have you thought of swapping or getting goods and services for free? The internet has spawned many websites to enable you to do this. If you are in trouble with a bank, mortgage provider or credit-card company, credit unions are a viable alternative to commercial banks and loan sharks. These not-for-profit organizations are a tried and tested method of banking, used by millions around the world. The World Council of Credit Unions is an international organization which will also tell you how to set up a credit union in your area.

Public money should be used for public good. Pressure your government to extend credit or loan guarantees that follow this principle. Meanwhile, anti-poverty and Drop the Debt campaigns need your support now more than ever.

7 What's FINANCE for?

To handle investment, measure risk and offer shelter from unpredictable adversity. Selling insurance, mortgages and pensions is all part of the work of financial services.

What has it become?

Bloated and unstable. In some countries, like Britain or Iceland, the financial services sector has grown so fast and so large that it overshadows the so-called 'real economy' of, say, manufacturing or retailing or other services. Finance has spawned an alphabet soup of complex 'products', including the notorious CDOs (or collateralized-debt-obligations) that triggered the current meltdown in the US. Much of the financial sector's business is about making bets, using powerful mathematical models that are all too fallible. Often it involves trading in things that do not actually exist (betting on the future price of copper, for example, or on who is going to default on credit). Though 'unreal', these activities cause extreme volatility in the share prices of otherwise viable companies, with devastatingly real consequences. The outcome for millions of people who – like it or not – have their pensions linked to the stock market, is lifetime savings lost and poverty in old age.

Does it have to be that way?
No. Just as financial services have been systematically deregulated and given perilous freedom, so they can be re-regulated. Financiers who have made fortunes from volatility resist regulation, saying only a 'light touch' is needed. But you have to question their motives. A big hit on the *Wall Street Journal* website is: 'How can I make money out of the credit crunch?'

What could be done?
Governments could impose an immediate and permanent global ban on 'short selling' of stocks and shares – an especially lethal form of trading in derivatives (contracts or financial instruments whose value is 'derived' from the value of something else, a commodity or mortgage, for example). The ban could be extended to all derivatives, unless they can prove some kind of social usefulness. Key areas that relate to people's basic needs – such as food – should be taken out of the arena of speculation.

The overweight financial services sector should go on a crash diet and the 'real economy' be boosted. The bonus culture that has done so much damage could be changed quite easily – by banning bonuses. Any received by executives in companies that have benefited from public bail-outs should be returned to the public purse, directly or indirectly. Executive salaries could be capped (following the lead of President Obama in the US). Commissions on the selling of financial products could be outlawed. Hiring more women in key positions might help feminize finance – the sector has been plagued by macho risk taking, fueled by the 'Big Swinging Dick' culture of trading floors. (One of the few investment banks that survived the Icelandic crash was run by women. Their policy was never to invest in anything they didn't understand.)

A radical rethink of pension policy is needed. Supposed to provide security in old age, pensions are the last thing that should be determined by the vagaries of the stock market. Britain's New Economics Foundation is proposing a 'People Pension' which would be better insulated from market turbulence than orthodox pension schemes. It would be backed by People's Pension Funds, with contributions invested in new public infrastructure projects such as schools, hospitals, transport and social housing.

What can I do?
Insist on people-centered finance that is tightly regulated and fully accountable. Some traders are claiming to have 'seen the light' and to be moving into new 'environmentally friendly' areas of activity, and therefore say they don't need regulating. Don't be fooled. Many are eyeing up the carbon trading market – itself an offspring of the ruinous financial markets. These speculators could well create another disastrous – albeit green – 'bubble'. Call for legal action against bankers, speculators, credit-rating agents and auditors, who misled clients and the public. In the US, hundreds of Wall Street bankers are currently being investigated for their part in the meltdown. Why not elsewhere?

8 What's THE ECONOMY for?
Housework. Seriously: the word economy derives from 'thrift' and 'administration' in 'managing a household'.

What's it become?

Worse than a teenager's bedroom. A globalized mess – built on over-production, over-consumption and unsustainable debt. Today's financial contagion has spread through the world's economies at such tremendous speed because the removal of trade barriers has made the system deeply interconnected. Governments, which since the 1980s have sold off public utilities to the private sector, are still loath to intervene, in spite of the market revealing its fatal flaws and limitations.

Does it have to be that way?

No. In fact, some less globalized countries, with more traditional banking sectors, may be able to weather the storm better than the export-led economies that are globalization's poster children.

What could be done?

So powerful and prevalent has been the faith in globalization that it seems almost heretical to suggest that what the world needs now is a dose of 'de-globalization'. Supporting production and consumption at a local or regional level is not only greener – it might also make a lot more economic sense. If governments, currently pouring billions into big failing banks, directed a fraction of this amount towards financing local enterprise, they could boost their economies and create jobs. The current crisis could bring key services and utilities back into public ownership, enabling greater accountability and democratic control. Instead of creating huge surpluses of goods, the focus could be on keeping a healthy balance between production and consumption. We could continue international trade, but give preference to eco-friendly and fairly traded items we need, rather than massive quantities of exploitatively produced things we don't really need. And if rich world governments devoted even a fraction of the money they have spent on saving private banks on international development aid they would meet the 0.7 per cent of GDP target of which most of them fall so far short. Perhaps we might then have a global economy that has people at its heart – rather than a finance-dominated one, that bets on the price of everything and knows the value of nothing.

What can I do?
One danger of the economic meltdown is that, as people tighten their belts, they become more selfish, thus squandering the opportunity for a badly needed shift in values. It's especially important to keep doing the things we believe in. If, for example, we value local shops, then we must use them or they will disappear. If we want an independent media or organic food or goods that are fairly traded then we need to maintain or increase our support for these things. The unraveling of consumer confidence is an opportunity for examining values and challenging assumptions – for example that economic growth is necessarily 'a good thing'. It's worth asking: 'What kind growth is good?' Growth in global finance, for example? For ideas and inspiration, check out the rapidly growing Transition Towns movement (www.transitiontowns.org) which has a worldwide membership.

9 What's TAXATION for?
To enable the state to raise money for public spending on, for example, health, education, transport... Under a progressive tax regime, the richer you are, the more tax you pay.

What's it become?
A transfer of wealth from the poor to the rich. If you are on a low or average income you have to pay tax and usually it's deducted at source; if you are rich you can avoid paying it altogether! Transnational corporations find it easy to hide profits in tax havens and use a range of arcane accounting practices to avoid paying tax. Some 60 per cent of world trade passes from one

corporate subsidiary or tax haven to another. Tax evasion in developing countries and capital flight from those countries is seven times greater than inflows of aid. The world's richest corporations or individuals – such as Rupert Murdoch's media empire or 'anti-poverty' campaigning musician Bono – pay little or no tax.

Does it have to be this way?
Of course not.

What could be done?
The rich could be made to pay more. Tax havens could be closed down – some of the most notorious are the British Crown dependencies such as Jersey, Cayman Islands and Virgin Islands. Loopholes, that make the US, Britain, Canada and Australia some of the easiest countries in which to avoid paying tax, should be closed. Good tax systems need transparency – no more secret Swiss bank accounts. All transactions – currency, shares and bonds – could be taxed. This would not only slow down speculative activity but could also raise considerable revenue, which could be directed towards meeting the Millennium Development Goals of halving world poverty by 2015. International trade too could be taxed (ignore howls of protests from the WTO). And for green taxes to work they need to be bold, environmentally effective and fiddle-proof. Windfall taxes would be payable by fossil-fuel companies – we could start with Shell and BP, both of which posted huge profits in early 2009.

What can I do?
Boycott banks with subsidiaries in tax havens (Citicorp, Barclays, Lloyds, HSBC, RBS, for example). Pressure your government to close down tax havens. If you are British, you can start close to home, in Jersey. Call for a closure of loopholes that enable most

large corporations to avoid paying billions of tax. Support people in developing countries who are trying to stop their élites from siphoning the countries' wealth into Western bank accounts. Check out the Tax Justice Network on www.taxjustice.net

10 What's THE ENVIRONMENT for?
Er... how about: it just *is?*

What's it become?
According to a capitalist and anthropocentric worldview, the environment is something to be exploited to extract maximum profit. It has become both a mine for natural resources and a dumping ground for waste.

Does it have to be that way?
No. Indigenous people have a far healthier approach, based on a give-and-take approach. This relationship involves respect for, and conservation of, the natural environment. Many in the West are trying to move towards aspects of this worldview.

What could be done?
Now is our big chance to do things differently. To develop production that is sustainable and eco-friendly. To back diverse forms of renewable energy. To put pressure on governments to transform their economies and create millions of new green jobs. At the time of writing, only one per cent of financial investment has been in green or ethical areas. All development and investment could be made to meet certain basic ecological criteria. We could identify and ring-fence the areas that are central to life and should never be privatized – water, major forests, the seas, the atmosphere. Mining and fossil fuels could be added to this. We could think about what we mean by 'the common interest'. Selfish, myopic short-termism has led us to the brink, environmentally as well as economically; a major

mindshift is required to think about future generations and act accordingly. We could start making that shift by separating two ideas that are often bound together as though they were one and the same – the notion of 'growth' and the notion of 'well-being'.

What can I do?
Keep in focus an issue that is even more significant than the turmoil in the global economy – climate change. Support renewable energy and join the resistance to new fossil fuel schemes like 'clean' coal or oil sands exploitation. Support those in developing countries who are trying to protect their environments from corporate plunder that will only hasten climate change. Oil exploration in the Amazon is an obvious case.

Closer to home, you can demand that your government commits to genuine, major domestic cuts (not offsets) in CO_2 emissions – and sticks to them.

This piece has drawn inspiration and ideas from many sources, not least the European Cross-Sectoral Networking Meeting of NGOs and activists organized by the S2B Network/Eurodad in Paris on 11 and 12 January 2009, the Put People First Coalition in Britain, and the World Social Forum 2009 meeting in Belém, Brazil. Peter Stalker's work on Global Finance (see page 97) and that of my colleagues in various issues of New Internationalist, *have also been very helpful.*

Vanessa Baird is a *New Internationalist* co-editor.

Connections: Ann Pettifor, p 21; Tarek El Diwany, p 85; Peter Stalker, p 97; George Monbiot, p 109; Patrick Bond, p 211.

PATRICK
OND

CHIVERS

DANNY

DEREK
WALL

MICHAEL
ALBERT

EVO
MORALES

NICOLA
BULLARD

WILK
KATE P.

The Trouble with Interest

Former derivatives trader Tarek El Diwany identifies the poison in our financial system – and suggests a cure.

I first applied for work in the City of London as a derivatives dealer in the late 1980s. Over casual chats I was informed that the City demanded a rare combination of intellect, eloquence and sharpness. Those in possession of this skill set would be rewarded handsomely, for the City was a place where talent was recognized, irrespective of age. So I was told, and it occurred to me that if I could succeed in this environment, then I would have proven my worth to the many doubting Thomases around me. A new Porsche 911 said so much more than mere words could.

Thus I acquiesced to the notion that success is measured by the amount of money that one earns. In the City I met many people who were fully committed to that notion, and who implemented it on a grand scale. Money was the sole measure of success. Make money, and you would be promoted. Fail to make money, and you would be sacked. Or moved to the training department. Financial products were invented and marketed not because they met a client need, but because they made an enormous profit for the bank or finance company. Research 'stories' were told in order to sell financial securities that insiders wouldn't touch with a barge pole. Massive gambles were taken with billions worth of depositors' funds, while in public the language of 'prudent banking' was dished out in solemn tones. Investment decisions were frequently made by people whose technical knowledge was shockingly poor, and sometimes for the flimsiest of reasons. 'Shares were up ten after a good lunch,' joked one of my bosses, and what a lunch it was!

I found that I was rather good at making money, although few of the financial theories that I had learned at university seemed to apply in my work. For example, the simplest laws of supply and demand didn't seem to work with regard to City salaries. If there were one hundred applicants for each City job, why did pay rates remain so obstinately high? If African countries were being told that good economic management meant running a balanced budget, why was it that the US and Britain, two of the most prosperous nations on earth, almost never ran a balanced budget? Even the cardinal rule of monetarism, that inflation could be reduced by raising the rate of interest, didn't make sense to me. The available data showed that a rise in interest rates actually had the opposite effect, by increasing the cost of mortgage repayments.

Despite my nagging doubts about the financial system, what eventually changed my perspective on the City were the attitudes and values that I encountered along the way. These undoubtedly rubbed off on me, but there comes a time when one is forced to make a choice between two ways of life. Clients were being treated as prey, when I wanted to treat them as human beings. Money had become a God, but I wanted to find out: 'Who is God? What does He expect of me?' This kind of talk was like death on the trading desk. It caused colleagues to go silent. Worse, it caused clients to stop ringing us.

Resigning one's post while at the top of the tree is almost unheard of in the City, but to do so in exchange for a career in Islamic finance was something that my colleagues found almost laughable. To me it offered the combination of ethics and profit that I had been looking for. For others, it represented an unacceptable interference by religion in the science of finance. Orthodox economists in particular liked to make that point. Religion was loaded with value judgements, they said, while economists dealt impartially with facts on the ground.

But such arguments overlooked the possibility that modern finance had itself become a religion. Here, the purpose of commercial activity was to maximize shareholder value, and the unit of measure was almost exclusively a monetary one. Stress, pollution, divorce and crime, all these could be conveniently ignored when measuring Gross Domestic Product. In this manner, a monetarily rich but unhappy society was seen as better off than a monetarily poor but happy one. Was this not a massive value judgement for modern finance to make?

As a newly practicing Muslim I discovered that the purpose of life is to worship the Creator, and that life is merely a test to determine whether we can fulfill that purpose. Wealth is a means for worshipping the Creator, not an end in its own right. To make the accumulation of wealth an objective of life is to worship wealth instead of the Creator, and this is one of the most fundamental errors that a human being can make. However, as in any test, we have the freedom to make that error. We can follow the commands of the Creator or ignore them and go our own way.

The responsibilities that the Creator requires us to fulfill include many that are understood by both religious and secular minds. If people are free to murder or steal from one another, if the one who has wealth does not pay the wealth tax, if the one who has power does not dispense it with justice, then the whole of society suffers. For any individual to enjoy a right, she or he must shoulder a corresponding responsibility, and the surest way to destroy human rights is for individuals to shirk their human responsibilities.

Among the responsibilities required of humankind, one above all has been relegated in the modern age. This is the prohibition of usury and it is common to the three Abrahamic faiths. However, unlike murder and theft, the destructive impact of usury is not always obvious and this has sustained much debate on the topic over many centuries in both East and West. For the Islamic jurist, usury encompasses a variety of commercial practices of which the fee charged by a moneylender is but one. Deuteronomy prohibits usury among the Jews, and the Gospel of Luke advises Christians to 'lend hoping for nothing thereby'. Indeed, the only violent act of Jesus' ministry was to expel the usurers from the temple, and as recently as 500 years ago those who profited from the act of lending money were committing a crime under English law.

Today everything has changed. The one who was despised in centuries past is now our financial overlord, inhabiting the plushest of city boardrooms. This remarkable transformation could not have been achieved without a heavy dose of legal semantics. In Rome during the early 13th century, Hispanus argued that while usury was surely prohibited, if a borrower was late in repaying a loan then the lender could charge a penalty fee. The period in between the date on which the borrower should have repaid and the date on which she or he did repay, Hispanus termed 'inter esse', that which 'in between is'. By the middle of the 16th century, Henry VIII permitted the charging of interest up to a rate of 10 per cent. Thus began the fall of the Christian prohibition of usury. Henceforth, only the practice of charging 'excessive' interest was to be proscribed.

The ability to practice usury was in olden times limited by the amount of gold or silver coins available to the moneylender. In the 17th century, a critical development in England largely removed this limiting factor. Here, early bankers took deposits of gold coins and in return issued paper receipts promising repayment on demand. In due course, merchants began to use the bankers' receipts in payment for goods and services. It was easier to hand over a paper receipt to a seller than to travel to the bank in order to withdraw coins first. This behavior allowed the bankers dramatically to enlarge their business as moneylenders because, from now on, when the public came to borrow money, the banker could lend them freshly printed paper receipts. This policy had one great advantage. Unlike gold, paper receipts could be manufactured at little or no cost. 'The Bank hath benefit of interest on all moneys which it creates out of nothing,' was how William Paterson, first Director of the Bank of England, put it in 1694. The more paper receipts bankers printed, the more loans they could make and the more interest they could earn. It was therefore 'in their interest' to create as much money as possible. But this policy had dire consequences for the rest of society. The more money that was issued into circulation, the more prices began to rise throughout the economy. And because every unit of paper money was issued under a loan contract, the indebtedness of society grew remorselessly over time. If a banker called in the paper loans, a vicious recession could easily result. The political power that this gave to the banks was not lost on President Andrew Jackson. In his farewell address of 1837, he accused the Bank of the United States of having done exactly this in an attempt to defeat his program of banking reform:

'The distress and alarm which pervaded and agitated the whole country when the Bank of the United States waged war upon the people in order to compel them to submit to its demands cannot yet be forgotten. The ruthless and unsparing temper with which whole cities and communities were oppressed, individuals impoverished and ruined, and a scene of cheerful prosperity suddenly changed into one of gloom and despondency ought to be indelibly impressed on the memory of the people of the United States. If such was its power in time of peace, what would it have been in a season of war, with an enemy at your doors? No nation but the free men [sic] of the United States could have come out victorious from such a contest; yet, if you had not conquered, the government would have passed from the hands of the many to the few, and this organized money power, from its secret conclave, would have dictated the choice of your highest officials and compelled you to make peace or war, as best suited their own wishes.'

If the banking classes favored men of similar inclinations with their loans of newly created money, a small group of individuals could quickly and quietly amass great influence over the commercial and political life of the nation. Today, this is a reality that extends into media and academia with devastating consequences at the intellectual level. Financial newspapers hesitate to publish material that is hostile to their largest source of advertising revenue, and the huge volumes of research and commentary that pour forth from researchers in the banking sector are similarly slanted by financial pressures. From cradle to grave, the issues of money creation and usury therefore tend to remain in the background, disguised by a terminology that is impenetrable to the lay person. As John Kenneth Galbraith wrote in *Money Whence it Came, Where it Went*: 'The study of money, above all other fields in economics, is the one in which complexity is used to disguise the truth or to evade the truth, not to reveal it.'

Nations across the world have thereby come to accept that interest-based debt is a normal fact of economic life. For most in the paradoxically labeled 'rich world', there is nothing dangerous or shameful in perpetual indebtedness. Our parents' advice to save for the things that we want in life is now mocked as an old-fashioned delusion. Why save, when the desire to consume can be satisfied now? Materialist ideologies reinforce such attitudes substantially. If there is no afterlife, then surely we must try to enjoy this life as much as possible?

Yet the inexorable rise of debt makes the enjoyment of life a distant dream for much of humanity. In the poorer countries, the objective becomes mere survival, if necessary by dint of politically spiked loan agreements. In 1997, the United Nations Development Programme estimated that up to five million children die in Africa every year because of the pressures that debt service places upon national budgets. Tanzania and Uganda were among many whose debt service payments exceeded the entire national budget for healthcare. The consequences of developing country indebtedness are ecological in nature too. For example, the fastest deforesting countries in the world are among its most indebted, as rainforests are sacrificed in order to earn the foreign exchange that will pay off creditors in the rich countries.

The model of borrowing funds at interest in order to invest and generate profit has now accumulated a long track record of failure in dealing with such problems. A glance at IMF figures on developing country debt tells a story of ever-climbing debt levels over five decades.

As for aid, the entire package of assistance given by the developed countries to the developing world is typically less than a quarter of the debt service payments that flow in the opposite direction. The widely trumpeted Heavily Indebted Poor Countries program of debt relief promoted

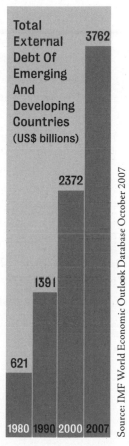

Total External Debt Of Emerging And Developing Countries (US$ billions)

3762

2372

1391

621

1980 1990 2000 2007

Source: IMF World Economic Outlook Database October 2007

91

by the IMF and World Bank in 1996 required widespread austerity budgets of the kind rarely implemented in the West, yet after more than a decade in operation only one nation out of 42 had been removed from the list of HIPC countries.

Underlying all of these problems is the practice of usury. In Islam, it is seen as fundamentally wrong for a financier to make a profit from a client even when that client's business is failing. Instead, the financier must share both the profits and the losses of those finances, much like modern equity investors do. This simple requirement ties together the interests of financiers and clients in a way that interest-based lending never can. When a financier can only make a profit if the client makes a profit, then the financier is much more careful about whom he finances. In interest-based finance, those who wish to obtain loan finance are often those who have the most collateral to offer, not those who have the best projects. Poor people with good business ideas therefore tend to stay poor under the interest-based system, precisely because they lack collateral and cannot therefore attract finance for their businesses.

The possibility of life without interest-based finance or money creation by a privileged élite is amply demonstrated by the history of Islamic empire. Here, profit-sharing, usury-free trade credit, charitable donations and *zakat* combined to fulfill the entire spectrum of society's needs. All of this was built upon the foundations of a commodity money system that held its purchasing power across centuries, where today's money cannot even hold its value across a single decade. Many of the great universities and hospitals of the Muslim world were funded by endowments, and much of its transport infrastructure from zakat funds. The modern private finance initiative cannot compete with these methods of financing. Interest charges typically devour at least a third of a project costing, with the result that today's infrastructure is a shadow of our former achievements. Just compare the flimsy modern extension to

London's St Pancras railway station with the beautiful original that John Betjeman helped save for the nation.

The fact that an alternative economic paradigm was once achieved in the Muslim world is a vital lesson for our time. It is therefore rather sad that instead of re-establishing that paradigm, modern Islamic financiers have rushed to adopt the institutional structures and product range of the interest-based world. Gone for now are the dreams of Islamic economists in the 1960s, who argued for a banking system that shared risk and reward with its clients. In its place we find an industry that camouflages interest-based loans with Islamic terminology and excuses its lack of vision by reference to the overarching realities of modern banking and finance.

The clients of banks, Islamic or otherwise, are not entirely passive actors in this tale of woe, for most of them have adopted interest-based leverage as the basis of their business activities. Why would an entrepreneur who makes a 20-per-cent profit on funds invested want to share that profit with investors, if he can finance himself using a loan at five-per-cent interest? And if borrowing $100 at five-per-cent interest allows a company to make $20 profit, then why not borrow $100 million and make $20 million in profit?

The inevitable commercial consequence of this mentality is that firms borrow as much as possible. In doing so, they can swallow up much of the competition and dominate their sector of the market. Interest-based leverage largely explains the tendency towards large-scale business operations throughout much of the Western world today. Five supermarkets now control more than 75 per cent of the British grocery trade, where 50 years ago thousands of independent retailers could be found competing with one another. In the fashion sector, although Dorothy Perkins, Burtons, BHS, Miss Selfridge, Top Man, Top Shop and Wallis compete for customers on many British high streets, this isn't quite the idyll of free market capitalism that first greets the eye. All of these shops are controlled by one retail tycoon, Philip Green, who lives his tax-free life in Monaco. In the construction sector the consequences of interest-based leverage are even more obvious. The beautiful towns and villages of yesteryear are being replaced with the anonymous housing estates that emanate from the drawing boards of massive corporations and bank mortgage departments. Housing has become a means not for building a community, but for extracting wealth from it. Thus, the financial resources that used to go towards making our buildings beautiful, now go to paying the interest charges and dividends of a few large corporations.

As independent owner-managed businesses decline in importance, the number of employees at or near the minimum wage is increasing dramatically. This feature alone has devastating consequences in terms of customer service and job satisfaction, for the one who owns her or his business tends to care much more for it than the one who works on a low wage and shares none of its success. Conveniently for those who proclaim the victory of modern finance capitalism, the resulting decline of morale among millions of British workers appears nowhere in our headline statistics on economic performance.

The above are just some of the features of life under the interest-based financial system. We should not have to live like this, but one small example from my own professional experience helps to demonstrate why we do. Some years ago our firm helped to develop and launch a radical new home-purchase scheme in Britain. It is based on a partnership arrangement in which a prospective home-buyer and financier together purchase a property as partners. The home-buyer may then occupy the property as a tenant, but can instead elect to rent the property to a third party. Both partners share any rental income and any capital gains or losses on the property price, in line with their partnership ratios, and the home-buyer may from time to time buy portions of the property from the financier at market value.

In this scheme, the home-buyer is never in debt for she or he has not borrowed money nor is required to buy the financier's share of the property. 'Negative equity', repossession and sleepless nights are a thing of the past under this approach to home finance.

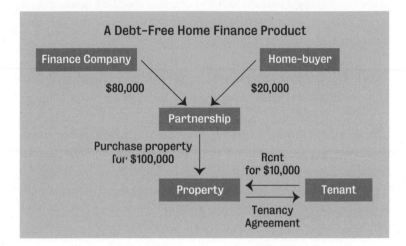

When we launched our product in London during 2005, we did so in the hope that it could be part of a wider solution for the reduction of household debt. Alas, we were met by a wall of silence from British financial institutions. Bankers, lawyers, consultants, brokers and property dealers, all were dipping their snouts in the trough of easy credit and were in no mood to adopt an alternative model of home finance. In this business, profits came from debt expansion, not debt reduction. This is precisely why those who have helped create the credit crisis should not be charged with finding a solution. To do so is to place the fox in charge of the chicken run.

As of late March 2009, trillions of newly created money has been fed to the banking industry in just a few months. It may prove hard to withdraw this money from circulation at a later date, in which case a historic hyperinflation is likely to ensue. This in turn will place the Western world but a few steps from dictatorship and war. It would be a brave person who bets against a financial establishment with a 300-year track record of survival, but if the interest-based monetary system is sustained it will be the cause of still greater crises and suffering in generations to come. Replacing it is therefore the critical struggle of our time. It is not a system we can reform. We must simply defeat it, because if we don't, it will defeat us.

Tarek El Diwany is a London-based financial advisor and founder of Zest Advisory LLP.

Connections: Ann Pettifor, p 21; Vanessa Baird, p 65; Peter Stalker, p 97.

RICHARD
WILKINSON &
KATE PICKETT
YASH
TANDON
BARBARA
EHRENREICH
JOHN
CHRISTENSEN
GEORGE
MONBIOT
PETER
STALKER

Starting Afresh

Money is too important to be left to bankers, whose greed and incompetence have resulted in a financial system capable of delivering them grotesque incomes but exposing everyone else to massive risk. Peter Stalker thinks it's time to start again, treating banking as a public utility that should be as tightly regulated as any other.

Banks exist for the simple purpose of connecting savers and borrowers, of making the best use of scarce resources.

Even in the traditional model there was an inherent risk in promising savers that they could withdraw their funds whenever they liked while simultaneously promising borrowers that they could keep the same funds for 20 years or more to build a business or buy a house. There was always the possibility that both groups would exercise their rights simultaneously, alarming investors and triggering a run on the bank. By and large this risk proved manageable. With sufficient guarantees of savings in place, and the capacity of the central bank to act as a lender of last resort, this scenario arose only rarely. In the UK the crisis in Northern Rock was the first major bank run in 90 years.

Over the last 20 years, however, a relatively straightforward financial model has become hugely more complex, as banks and other financial institutions have devised ever more intricate interlocking forms of investment and borrowing. They would argue that they have done so in order to respond to market demand, creating opportunities for investors and borrowers that offer different combinations of cost and risk to meet every need – from those of the pensioners trying to conserve their nest eggs to those high-rolling hedge fund gamblers willing to stake millions of dollars in a single transaction. The consequences included steep rises in stock and property prices – very welcome to those who owned stocks or houses, even if they did not appreciate how this boom could lead to a massive bust.

Governments, who should have known better, have largely stood aside, and have chosen to deregulate the financial sector – giving the bankers free rein to dream up multiple new schemes, however impenetrable. The financial sector was also a rich source of income. In the UK, the Government welcomed a steady flow of funds via taxation: by 2004 the financial sector, although constituting only one-tenth of national output, was contributing more than one-quarter of corporation tax revenues. Then there was the income tax from all those high-earning traders. Between 1997 and 2006, the number of people earning over $100,000, many of whom worked in the City of London, had risen to 500,000, increasing their tax contribution over the same period from $10 billion to $34 billion – from 13 per cent to one-quarter of all income tax revenue.[1]

This gives the mistaken impression that the financiers are creating new wealth. In reality they are just taking other people's money. If you save or borrow through a building society or a credit union or any other form of mutual system, you will get a lower savings rate than is charged to borrowers – there is always a 'spread'. This is understandable, since the organization that brings savers and borrowers together has to pay administration and wage costs. The financial services industry, for all its presumed sophistication, ultimately does much the same thing, except that it multiplies the number of intermediaries and their salaries – and therefore the spread. From hedge funds to investment banks they are doing the same thing as a credit union, borrowing and lending, but by devising many new ways of gathering and dispersing money they have been able to grab more of the spread for themselves.

The value that underpins financial earnings depends finally on workers and entrepreneurs operating businesses to provide goods and services. Over the longer term this has created 'real' returns in the stock market of around five per cent per year. In recent years, however, the financial services industry has been taking a larger cut of this. This has been termed the 'croupier's take' – the amount skimmed off by investment banks, by various brokers, traders, operators of mutual funds, and financial advisers, who between them grab between 40 and 80 per cent of the money that might otherwise have gone to investors.[2]

This dense thicket of transactions is usually justified on the grounds that it meets with exquisite precision the needs of borrowers and investors, as perfect financial markets respond to subtle shifts in supply and demand. But the financial markets are far from perfect. No-one knows fully what is going on, even in publicly traded shares. However, some participants have insider information: corporate managers and the traders have a far better idea than investors – an imbalance referred to as 'asymmetry of information' – and use this to their own advantage.

Another justification for all this financial innovation is that everyone is free to assume the degree of risk with which they are comfortable. Again this is a myth. Few people are capable of accurately assessing risk. Even the directors of investment funds have only the vaguest idea what their own staff are up to, and don't much care, as long as this month's profit figures are good. Governments too have been somewhat in awe of the financial wizards and have been proud of applying a light regulatory touch, arguing that the most dangerous arenas of speculation affect only sophisticated investors who know what they are doing and need little protection. As has become abundantly clear, however, while the high-rollers are willing to monopolize the rewards of success, they have been more generous with the fruits of failure – forcing governments into rescue acts to stave off systemic collapses.

Much is made of the complexity and ingenuity of modern financial models. Perhaps judged by their own criteria they are sophisticated. But in fact complexity is often a sign of incompetence. Any computer programmer knows that it takes only two or three inept lines of code to generate unpredictable outcomes – and cause a computer to freeze. Similarly, some relatively straightforward operations on a ball of wool by the average cat will rapidly produce an almighty tangle of which the cat can be very proud. The global financial system is in a comparable mess, and is unsafe in the hands of bankers.

What are the alternatives? There can be no single answer but there are at least some measures that would steer finance in a more productive direction.

Revoke licenses to print money
One of the more remarkable features of the financial system is that most of the money is made by banks. This is not just because they can make huge profits, but because they do create most of the money. Assuming that banks keep only 10 per cent of each deposit and lend the rest, then for each $100 deposited they add a further $900 to the stock of money. A fundamental reorganization of global monetary systems should start at this point. A number of theorists have pointed out that allowing banks to create money is fundamentally unjust since it involves a massive and continuing transfer of resources from the public to the private sector.

Monarchs and other rulers originally had the monopoly on issuing new money in the form of coins. Then private and later central banks stepped in, by issuing new coins and paper money. Governments could spend this into circulation, for example, by using it to pay soldiers or government officials. This privilege, of being able to make money and spend it, is known as 'seignorage'.

Nowadays, however, coins and banknotes account for only around five per cent of the new money that appears. The rest materializes, as if by magic, when commercial banks make loans to their customers. The amount they can lend is limited only by how much of their own capital they retain to offset bad debts. In the past they have usually been happy to lend around ten times their capital, though in current circumstances this ratio has been reduced to seven or eight.[3]

The other creator of money is the central bank. In the UK for example, according to monetary theorist James Robertson, the government issues around $6 billion per year in coins and banknotes which it uses to pay its own bills. But this is dwarfed by the money created and extinguished by banks which earns them around $40 billion per year in profits. If, on the other hand, new money for the British financial system could be created only by the Bank of England and spent into circulation by the government, this would provide it with $90 billion a year to spend.[4] In other countries a similar system would be equivalent to $114 billion in the US, €160 billion in the euro area, and more than ¥17 trillion in Japan. These amounts are equivalent to between 5 and 15 per cent of tax revenues, enabling governments to boost public expenditure, cut taxes or distribute money to every citizen in the form of income entitlements.

Practicalities

How would this work? It would primarily require making a sharp distinction between the money in your current account for transactions and the money in savings accounts. In this new system when you put money into your current account (a 'sight deposit') this would act as a sort of holding box and thus pay no interest. As now, you could use the money to pay bills, either in cash or electronically. But this money would not appear on the balance sheet of the banks; it would be money that belongs to you, just like banknotes in your wallet.

Banks would continue to offer loans, but they would do so in a much simpler fashion. Anything they lend would have to come from money deposited with them by savers, or borrowed from other banks, or from their tills, or from their own accounts held at the central bank. In total this would not greatly change the functioning of banks but it would oblige them to operate in a more transparent fashion and under greater government control. They would continue to offer services, for a suitable fee, and make loans but would not be able to cream off extra profits by creating money.

This reform would also result in greater economic stability. For example, during an economic downturn bank customers tend to stop taking new loans, or will pay off old ones. In the existing system, just as creating new loans increases the stock of money, so paying off old ones diminishes it. Less money in circulation then tends to make the recession even worse, sending the economy on a downward spiral of deflation. In short, by lending money commercial banks tend to amplify both the peaks and troughs. But if the supply of money is effectively fixed by the central bank then as people repaid loans they would simply return it to its original owners so the stock of money would be unchanged.

Return to savings
In addition, there should be other changes in the ways in which banks operate. In the relentless pursuit of profits banks have grown dissatisfied with the model of simply gathering funds from savers and instead have turned to the wholesale money markets either to borrow the funds for mortgages and other loans or to securitize mortgages. The British bank Northern Rock pursued this strategy relentlessly and recklessly on the assumption that it could roll over its loans from the money

markets whenever it wished. When the big lenders started to say no, everything fell to pieces.

Instead, banks should be required to make a much higher proportion of loans from deposits, and rather than securitizing them they should keep them on their own balance sheets so that both their customers and depositors are fully aware of the bank's situation. This would mean shifting from the originate-to-distribute model back to the originate-to-hold model. Banks also need to ensure that they retain sufficient capital – to be accumulated during boom years, rather than being paid out as huge bonuses or dividends, and held in reserve for economic downturns.

The financial meltdown has also raised questions about the ownership of banks. The whole or part nationalization of banks may have appeared surprising in free market economies in Europe and the United States. But this simply revealed an underlying truth that by operating with implicit or explicit state guarantees, banks are necessarily under the protective umbrella of national treasuries. The logical solution would be for banks to stay nationalized, or at least for some banks to remain in state hands to offer depositors and borrowers a different option. This would make it more difficult for the other banks to compete, as the subsequent success of the nationalized Northern Rock has demonstrated. So much the better.

Size matters

Another issue is the size of commercial banks. One of the legacies of the meltdown of 2008 is that it has resulted in a series of bank takeovers, as the ones still standing seized the opportunity to absorb those at death's door. The British Government swatted away concerns about competition when it encouraged LloydsTSB to take over HBOS. Part of the problem with banks is that most have grown too big to be allowed to fail. Instead they should be broken up so that none is large enough for its failure to pose a systemic risk. While the deposits of customers should be guaranteed, the survival of the bank should not be.

Even more alarming is that investment banks have become increasingly merged with retail banks into 'universal banks'. In the US, this has involved some retail banks taking over investment banks and some investment banks applying for retail banking licenses. This is precisely the wrong direction. The two functions should be kept entirely separate since this puts retail depositors at risk when the investment arm gets into trouble or, more likely, cries for help to the weary taxpayer.

In all of this, bank customers should have the choice of which institutions to use – either a state-owned bank offering the greatest security, or a reasonably sized and well run commercial bank, or a credit union, or more likely a mixture of one or more.

Prune the exotica

The meltdown of 2008 and the ensuing economic recession it triggered can be laid firmly at the door of speculators in banks, hedge funds and other institutions who had created a shadow financial system, operating with intertwining and overlapping derivatives. Not only were these barely comprehended, even by those using them, the ways in which they would interact were almost impossible to predict. Some derivatives are useful; others are largely vehicles for speculation. All should be presented for inspection by the financial authorities and only those approved should be used – and traded on public exchanges so that everyone is aware of who owns what and which institution is exposed to what risk. Trading in unapproved derivatives would be stifled if these were legally unenforceable.

Among the most dangerous derivatives are credit default swaps, currently valued at around $55 trillion – an indirect and opaque form of insurance that could yet sink many more lenders.[5] These should be banned, requiring lenders to take full responsibility for the credit they offer and denying speculators this particular form of get-rich scheme.

Also in line for pruning should be the hedge funds. At present these are largely unregulated since it was wrongly assumed they were a risk only to themselves. One way to reduce the damage would be to prevent short selling by banning other institutions from lending them the shares they need for this purpose.

Tax the transactions

Distortions and bubbles of all kinds are encouraged by electronic trading, which can see shares or currencies or bonds changing hands continuously at lightning speed. This encourages 'momentum' trading which has nothing to do with underlying values and more to do with what other traders will do in the subsequent seconds or minutes. One of the most promising ways of addressing this, but as yet untried 30 years after it was proposed by Nobel laureate James Tobin, would be to tax every transaction. At present only around five per cent of currency trades, around $3 trillion per day, are linked to actual trade. The rest is speculation which can wreak havoc with national budgets, especially for developing countries.

Applying a sales tax of around 0.2 per cent on each trade would skim off much of the speculative froth – while also generating valuable revenue. Assuming the annual trade were cut to a more reasonable level of $100 trillion this would yield tax revenues of $200 billion for public purses. The same principle could be applied to stock exchanges, which would have the merit of stifling some of the endless churning of stocks in hedge funds which achieve little other than to enrich traders and brokers.

Match risks and rewards

The most repulsive aspect of the 2008 financial crisis is that even disgraced chief executives of failed banks walked away with huge bonuses, as reward for failure. This is because the incentive systems encouraged employees to take bets on the markets that would produce short-term gains, in risky deals and crazy loans that would later turn toxic, by which time the trader or chief executive would have collected millions of dollars. This is akin to betting against a number coming up on a roulette wheel – you can take quite a few spins before being caught out, by which time you could have moved on to a different game. When chief executive Stan O'Neal was ousted from Merrill Lynch in October 2007, he was comforted with a $160-million pay-off, in part based on a rise in the share price that had yet to reflect his dangerous strategies. The pay for bankers and others should be based instead on continuous assessment of their performance and, where appropriate, reflect the full implications of their activities, even if these may not be known for several years. This will mean devising new contracts, so now's a good time while the bankers are looking for jobs and are not so picky about the perks.

Close tax havens
The world's tax havens serve no purpose other than to boost corporate profits and rich individuals at the expense of regular taxpayers. The British Government bears much of the responsibility since it is in a position to exert direct control over some of its own territories.[6] But there are other measures that could be taken to lift the veil of secrecy under which many companies and individuals operate, as they shuffle money from one dubious jurisdiction to another. This would involve, for example, demanding that companies declare the profits, losses, and taxes they pay in every country they do business. Just as important would be to end banking secrecy and ensure that tax authorities in each country are able to exchange the necessary information.

A fresh start
The 2008 financial meltdown has had huge costs, not just for taxpayers in the rich countries but also for millions of people in

developing countries who are suffering from a global economic crisis. But it also represents an opportunity for a fresh start – looking again at the most basic assumptions under which our financial systems operate.

The corporate lobbyists are, of course, busy preparing their arguments as to why it would be dangerous to react to the latest drama by stifling the creativity of financial markets. They claim that the latest crisis is simply part of a cycle of creative destruction, a Darwinian process that will permit the survival of the most robust financial models and sweep away those that have proved useless or dangerous.

But we now know the true cost of this free-for-all. The financial markets are not to be trusted. They expect to be given free rein to make huge profits while the sun is shining, but hasten to the shelter of the state when the skies darken. Never again. We now know better. Time to devise a new financial architecture.

This is an extract from The No-Nonsense Guide to Global Finance, *New Internationalist Publications, 2009.*

Peter Stalker, a former co-editor of *New Internationalist*, is a freelance author, editor and web designer. www.pstalker.com

Connections: Ann Pettifor, p 21; Vanessa Baird, p 65; Tarek El Diwany, p 85; George Monbiot, p 109; John Christensen, p 115; Yash Tandon p 131.

1 Giles, C and S de Daneshkhu, 'City of London offsets Budget tax shortfall', in *The Financial Times*, 26 March 2006. 2 Ford, J, 'A greedy giant out of control', in *Prospect*, November 2008. 3 'The end of the affair', in *The Economist*, 22 November 2008. 4 Huber, J and J Robertson, *Creating new money: A monetary reform for the information age*, New Economics Foundation, London, 2000. 5 Tricks, H, 'Dirty words', in *The World in 2009*, The Economist, London, 2008. 6 Mathiason, N and H Stewart, 'Obama backs crackdown on tax havens', in *The Observer*, 9 November 2008.

DAVID
NSOM

JOHN
HILARY

PATRICK
BOND

DANNY
CHIVERS

DEREK
WALL

MICHAEL
ALBERT

E...
MORAL...

NICOLA
WILLARD
RICHARD
KATE PICKETT
WILKINSON &
YASH
TANDON
BARBARA
EHRENREICH
CHRISTENSEN
JOHN
GEORGE
MONBIOT

Making Money

George Monbiot discovers some useful currencies of a rather different kind.

In Russell Hoban's novel *Riddley Walker*, the descendants of nuclear holocaust survivors seek amid the rubble the key to recovering their lost civilization. They end up believing that the answer is to re-invent the atom bomb. I was reminded of this when I read the [British] Government's plans to save us from the credit crunch. It intended – at gob-smacking public expense – to persuade the banks to start lending again, at levels similar to those of 2007. Wasn't this what caused the problem in the first place? Were insane levels of lending really the solution to a crisis caused by insane levels of lending?

Yes, I know that without money there's no business, and without business there are no jobs. I also know that most of the money in circulation is issued, through fractional reserve banking, in the form of debt. This means that you can't solve one problem (a lack of money) without causing another (a mountain of debt). There must be a better way than this.

This isn't my subject and I am venturing way beyond my pay grade. But I want to introduce you to another way of negotiating a credit crunch, which requires no moral hazard, no hair of the dog and no public spending. I'm relying, in explaining it, on the former currency trader and central banker Bernard Lietaer.

In his book *The Future of Money*, Lietaer points out that in situations like ours everything grinds to a halt for want of money. But he also explains that there is no reason why this money should take the form of sterling or be issued by the banks. Money consists only of 'an agreement within a community to use something as a medium of exchange'.[1] The medium of exchange could be anything, as long as everyone who uses it trusts that everyone else will recognize its value. During the Great Depression, businesses in the United States issued rabbit tails, seashells and wooden discs as currency, as well as all manner of papers and metal tokens. In 1971, Jaime Lerner, the Mayor of Curitiba in Brazil, kick-started the economy of the city and solved two major social problems, by issuing currency in the form of bus tokens. People earned them by picking and sorting litter: thus cleaning the streets and acquiring the means to commute to work. Schemes like this helped Curitiba become one of the most prosperous cities in Brazil.

But the projects which have proved most effective were those inspired by the German economist Silvio Gesell, who became finance minister in Gustav Landauer's doomed Bavarian republic. He proposed that communities seeking to rescue themselves from economic collapse should issue their own currency. To discourage people from hoarding it, they should impose a fee (called demurrage), which had the same effect as negative interest. The back of each banknote would contain 12 boxes. For the note to remain valid, the owner had to buy a stamp every month and stick it in one of the boxes. It would be withdrawn from circulation after a year. Money of this kind is called stamp scrip: a privately issued currency which becomes less valuable the longer you hold onto it.

One of the first places to experiment with this scheme was the small German town of Schwanenkirchen. In 1923, hyperinflation had caused a credit crunch of a different kind. A Dr Hebecker, owner of a coalmine in Schwanenkirchen, told his workers that if they wouldn't accept the coal-backed stamp scrip he had invented – the Wara – he would have to close the mine. He promised to exchange it, in the first instance, for food. The scheme immediately took off. It saved both the mine and the town. It was soon adopted by 2000 corporations across Germany. But in 1931, under pressure from the central bank, the ministry of finance closed the project down, with catastrophic consequences for the communities which had come to depend on it. Lietaer points out that the only remaining option for the German economy was ruthless centralized economic planning. Would Hitler have come to power if the Wara and similar schemes had been allowed to survive?

The Austrian town of Wörgl also tried out Gesell's idea, in 1932. Like most communities in Europe at the time, it suffered from mass unemployment and a shortage of money for public works. Instead of spending the town's meager funds on new works, the mayor put them on deposit as a guarantee for the stamp scrip he issued. By paying workers in the new currency, he paved the streets, restored the water system and built a bridge, new houses and a ski jump. Because they would soon lose their value, Wörgl's own schillings circulated much faster than the official money, with the result that each unit of currency generated 12 to 14 times more employment. Scores of other towns sought to copy the scheme, at which point – in 1933 – the central bank stamped it out. Wörgl's workers were thrown out of work again.

Similar projects took off at the same time in dozens of countries. Almost all of them were closed down as the central banks panicked about losing their monopoly over the control of money (just one, Switzerland's WIR system, still exists).

Roosevelt prohibited complementary currencies by executive decree, though they might have offered a faster, cheaper and more effective means of pulling the US out of the Depression than his New Deal.

No-one is suggesting that we replace official currencies with local scrip: this is a complementary system, not an alternative. Nor does Lietaer propose this as a solution to all economic ills. But even before you consider how it could be improved through modern information technology, several features of Gesell's system grab your attention. We need not wait for the government or the central bank to save us: we can set this system up ourselves. It costs taxpayers nothing. It bypasses the greedy banks. It recharges local economies and gives local businesses an advantage over multinationals. It can be tailored to the needs of the community. It does not require – as Eddie George, the former Governor of the Bank of England, insisted – that one part of the country be squeezed so that another can prosper.

Perhaps most importantly, a demurrage system reverses the ecological problem of discount rates. If you have to pay to keep your money, the later you receive your income, the more valuable it will be. So it makes economic sense, under this system, to invest long-term. As resources in the ground are a better store of value than money in the bank, the system encourages their conservation.

I make no claim to expertise. I'm not qualified to identify the flaws in this scheme, nor am I confident that I have made the best case for it. All I ask is that, if you haven't come across it before, you don't dismiss it before learning more. As we confront the failure of the Government's first bail-out and the astonishing costs of the second, isn't it time we considered the alternatives?

George Monbiot is an environmental activist, author and columnist for *The Guardian*. His most recent book is *Heat: How to stop the planet burning*, Allen Lane, London, 2006.

1 Bernard Lietaer, *The Future of Money*, Century, London, 2001.

Connections: Vanessa Baird, p 65; Peter Stalker, p 97; Derek Wall, p 181.

ANN
'TTIFOR

DAVID
RANSOM

JOHN
HILARY

PATRICK
BOND

DANNY
CHIVERS

DEREK
WALL

MIL
ALBER

Can Pay, Won't Pay

Much of the world's wealth now hangs out in tax havens, as John Christensen knows from first-hand experience. The consequences have been disastrous. But the winds of financial crisis, which the havens helped to fuel, might finally be about to blow them away.

It was a hot, windless afternoon in August 1995 and the atmosphere in my office in Saint Helier, Jersey, was stifling. I was economic adviser to this Channel Island tax haven, one of many offshore satellites of the City of London, and I was sitting opposite a multi-millionaire and his wife and their six financial and legal advisers. I asked him why he had not paid a penny of income tax in five years. His defense was this: my millionaire friends pay no tax and my financial advisers told me I do not need to pay tax – so why should I?

His defense could almost be a manifesto for the world's wealthy: 'We're rich, we're different – and taxes are for the little people.'

The millionaire's team were stunned by my pugnacious attitude: this was not the Jersey way. I asked him: 'Which of your advisers said you need not pay tax?' I saw a banker flinch, and hold his hands up to his face. It was him.

Later, out of curiosity, I checked his claim about Jersey's super-wealthy – and he was largely right. Many, I found, paid astonishingly little tax or, in more than half the cases I examined, nothing at all.

The world's super-rich have set themselves apart from the rest of society and have created a vast offshore economy from where they, and powerful corporations, can disengage from regulation and taxes, leaving the rest of us to pay the bills. This was the secret parallel universe I set out to research in the 1980s. Living in Jersey gave me the perfect cover.

A few figures help illuminate the rot. Since financial market deregulation in the 1980s the number of tax havens has more than trebled. Over $600 billion – nearly three times today's external debt – has leaked from sub-Saharan Africa in capital flight since 1975, almost all disappearing into secret bank accounts and offshore companies in places like Jersey, Luxembourg, Switzerland and London.

The scale of this scandal is mind-boggling. Conservative estimates suggest that the world's wealthiest individuals have parked $11.5 trillion offshore – allowing them to dodge over $250 billion dollars each year in tax. That alone far exceeds what the UN asked for in its Millennium project to tackle global poverty.

But that is just part of the picture: tax dodging by corporations is much, much bigger. The World Bank has reported that cross-border flows of the proceeds from criminal activities, corruption and tax evasion range from $1 trillion to $1.6 trillion per year, with half (or $500 to $800 billion) coming from Majority World economies. The rich countries currently spend about $100 billion on aid. So for every dollar of aid in, five to eight dollars flow out under the table. The tax evasion component of the global sum is by far the biggest, with commercial tax evasion making up $700 to $1,000 billion of the global figure. Historically there has not been such a large gap between rich and poor – ever.

Anyone who has worked in Majority World countries will have encountered the widespread public perception that wealth, especially wealth from minerals and natural resources like timber, but also development assistance funding and external debt, has been expropriated by corrupt political and business élites and exported to offshore bank accounts and trusts in tax havens like Switzerland, Monaco, the Cayman Islands and Jersey. The corrosive combination of huge inequality and social exclusion in these countries has nurtured deep tensions, most notably in the oil-exporting countries, where fabulous wealth has been accumulated by tiny élites while the majority of the population is unemployed and lives in appalling poverty. That poverty fosters crime, fueling violence and increasing the attraction of terrorism. Viewed from this perspective, the link between dirty-money flows into offshore bank accounts and widespread resentment of the West in so many poor countries becomes easier to understand.

The almost ceaseless looting of Nigeria's assets and that country's continuing slide toward gangsterism and violence vividly illustrates the problem. According to the *Economist* magazine: 'When Sani Abacha was dictator of Nigeria at the end of the 1990s, the Central Bank [of Nigeria] had a standing order to transfer $15 million or so to his Swiss bank account every day.' Embezzlement on this scale is not possible without an extensive pinstripe-suited infrastructure of financial specialists and offshore government officials who profit by providing an interface between crime and mainstream financial systems. Approximately 100 banks around the world were involved in handling Abacha's loot, including major names like Citigroup, HSBC, BNP Paribas, Credit Suisse, Standard Chartered, Deutsche Morgan Grenfell, Commerzbank and the Bank of India. According to Raymond Baker, an expert on money laundering at the Washington-based Center for International Policy: 'With a fortune estimated at $3 billion to $5 billion, a feeding frenzy arose to receive, shelter and manage Abacha's wealth.'[1]

About $300 million of Abacha's ill-gotten loot ended up in Jersey-based banks, which would undoubtedly have known the origin of this money and charged top dollar for managing funds on behalf of such a politically exposed person ('PEP'). Needless to say, when international pressure finally forced the repatriation of this looted money to Nigeria after Abacha's downfall, not a cent of this fee income was repaid, and not a single white-collar criminal was indicted – let alone punished in any way – for having aided and abetted one of the most flagrant crimes in Africa's recent history. Instead, the Jersey authorities trumpeted loudly about how virtuous they had been in repatriating the money.

Jersey, and other tax havens like it, provides an offshore interface that connects the regulated with the unregulated and the licit with the illicit. Superficially, the offshore banking world appears to mimic the onshore, but the lack of transparency and accountability means that offshore companies are not audited, there is no way of knowing who owns those companies, who benefits from the offshore trusts and what purpose they serve. This provides an ideal setting for criminality and corruption to become indistinguishable from the mainstream economy. Companies do not use tax havens to add economic value to their activities but as a means of economic 'free riding' or carrying out a financial scam. Operating in a tax haven involves participating in the globalized economy of fraud, corruption, money laundering, tax evasion, arms trafficking, mafia racketeering, insider trading and other forms of market distortion that tilt the playing field away from genuine enterprise and wealth creation.

Put simply, corruption on the scale of hundreds of billions of dollars annually in the Global South cannot survive without the complicity of wealthy countries' financial institutions. Nigeria has consistently topped Transparency International's international corruption index, but it is hard to disagree with Professor Aliya Fafunwa, a former Nigerian education minister, when he said in 2005 that Switzerland should top the list of most corrupt nations 'for harboring, encouraging and enticing robbers of public treasuries around the world to bring their loot for safe keeping in their dirty vaults'.[2]

Alongside the tax evasion, corruption, and embezzlement by local élites, it is also clear that international trade and investment flows have been shaped to make extensive use of tax havens for tax-dodging purposes. Jersey, for example, has been used for many years to import primary commodities like bananas and coffee to Europe. Of course, neither of these tropical crops could actually grow in the cold and windy English Channel, but on paper this trade passes through Jersey, partly in order to shift the profits offshore but also to disguise the true ownership of the companies involved in this trade, and to avoid disclosing the extent to which these markets have become dominated by a handful of oligopolistic businesses. The British Government has estimated that at least half of all world trade now passes – on paper – through tax havens, so the scale of profit laundering is immense.

Why has the tax haven racket been allowed to flourish this long? Havens lie at the heart of global financial markets – with over $2 trillion flowing daily through their circuits. Yet their role in undermining regulation and destroying the integrity of national tax systems is poorly understood. Efforts to tackle the problem have been pitiful and fiercely resisted, as was evident to observers of the April 2009 G20 Summit in London.

Lawyers, accountants and bankers working for the super-rich have helped develop new legal and financial structures and have strong-armed governments into setting up lax regulatory and tax frameworks. Meanwhile, major OECD nations, including Austria, Luxembourg, Switzerland, Britain and the US, have actively hindered reform, while civil society has mostly shied away from the issue because of its complexity.

London has become the largest offshore financial center.

In the 1950s, during decolonization, Britain was trailing on competitiveness and investment and the City was stagnant. Decolonization allowed Britain to create a network of quasi-autonomous states to funnel capital flows towards London. Almost half the world's tax havens, including the Cayman Islands, the Channel Islands, the British Virgin Islands and Bermuda, have close political ties to Britain, and they host some of the most substantial offshore financial centers, largely staffed by expatriate specialists originating from the City. But Britain denies it is a tax haven.

By encouraging its overseas territories and Crown dependencies to become tax havens, the British Government set in motion a global financial octopus with the City as its head, heart and mouth, and the satellite tax havens as its tentacles, scooping up vast sums of money from around the world and feeding it into London.

The latest recruit is Ghana, a Commonwealth country which, at the prompting of British banking giant Barclays, announced in 2007 its plans to transform Accra into a tax haven. Given the porous borders in the West African region, and the huge illicit wealth flows arising from oil, diamonds and other minerals in the region, it doesn't require much imagination to see how toxic this tax haven is likely to be for regional development.

Britain and British banks are not the only culprits, of course: we all know about the massive tax evasion scandal that has rocked Liechtenstein since early 2008. A similar scandal has engulfed Swiss private banking giant UBS, which has been required by a US Court to provide information relating to the accounts of 52,000 wealthy US citizens suspected of using that bank for tax evasion purposes. Singapore is energetically attracting dirty money from Asia and Europe. US states like Delaware and Miami have tax haven characteristics, which allow wealthy people, especially from Latin America, to disguise their identity when they invest in US Treasury Bonds. With more countries getting in on the act, a process of 'tax competition' between jurisdictions has emerged, as each competes to offer incentives to footloose capital. Secrecy and lax regulation serve as the major lures. In April 2008, for example, Jersey set up its first unregulated hedge fund. Others will follow. In the 1990s the OECD tried to address the scandal with its 'harmful tax competition' project, but the initiative was neutered by financial lobbies and President George W Bush's incoming administration.

Powerful companies and super-wealthy people – backed by a pinstripe infrastructure of financial intermediaries – have ruthlessly exploited this race to the bottom. Even the most powerful nations cannot resist the pressures. 'Cut our taxes,' company directors demand, 'or we will move to Ireland, or Switzerland.' 'Give us special treatment on capital gains,' the private equity magnates warn, 'or we will invest our wealth elsewhere.' National governments quail before these threats – and concede to the plutocrats. And the race continues.

The outcome has been disastrous. Tax havens have played a major part in the current crisis. They have been used for a variety of purposes, including:

- to create complex securitized instruments (mostly collateralized debt obligations) to mix packages of risk that have been marketed indiscriminately around the world
- to register 'off-balance sheet' entities that have been used to withhold materially sensitive information from investors, regulators, rating agencies, journalists and others
- to degrade the regulatory regimes of other nation states
- to create complex and opaque structures criss-crossing multiples of jurisdictions in order to confuse investigation and fragment regulatory effort to evade and avoid tax on an industrial scale.

In other words, tax havens have become engines of chaos in the financial markets, serving the dual purposes of helping financiers to 'get-out-of taxation-free' and also 'get-out-of regulation-free'.

In a world of global banks and 24-hour financial markets, regulation is only as effective as the weakest link in the chain: tax havens are the weakest link. This explains why so much of the 'financial innovation' of the past two decades can be traced back to these places. The majority of hedge funds are located in London, the Cayman Islands and the British Channel Islands. Ditto the private equity industry, the issuance of securitized debt, the re-insurance industry and the structured investment vehicles at the heart of the shadow banking system.

The current crisis did not arise solely from the sub-prime mortgage market failure in the US: it arose because financiers have created a shadow economy that is so opaque in its operations, so complex in its structure and so aggressively antagonistic towards democracy, regulation and taxation, that no-one can or should trust any of its activities.

De-regulation of financial markets in the 1980s opened the door for tax and regulatory competition. Tax competition has been used to increase returns to capital and, by lowering government revenues, to force privatization of strategic assets. De-regulation has greatly increased profitability, but at massive cost to workers, consumers and the environment. Tax havens have been used as mechanisms for catalyzing both processes, acting as termites which hollow out the structures designed to protect society from predatory practices.

To all intents and purposes, tax havens represent a financial world without rules, where criminality can prosper. My own experiences of working in Jersey suggest that the secrecy they provide facilitates not just tax evasion, but also insider dealing, market rigging, payment of illicit political donations, non-disclosure of conflicts of interest, facilitation of bribery and all sorts of other corrupt practices. And this happens day in, day out on an industrial scale.

Across the world the tax charge has been shifted from those who can afford it, powerful companies and rich people, onto workers and consumers: the inevitable outcome has been less job creation, greater inequality and rising poverty rates. This is especially a curse on poor countries, but not only on them: former US Treasury Secretary Larry Summers recently noted that if the income distribution in the US were the same today as in 1979, the poorest 80 per cent of Americans would have about $670 billion more – or about $8,000 per family – while the top one per cent would have about $670 billion less, or about $500,000 per family.

The economics profession and the aid industry, among others, have largely ignored this vast offshore economy. Most orthodox economists don't even identify the offshore economy as a political or economic phenomenon, let alone ask why over half of world trade passes – on paper – through tax havens. The World Bank and the IMF have failed to incorporate into their analyses how tax havens destabilize financial markets by allowing risks to be disguised in complex offshore structures, or to explore systematically their role in driving inequality and poverty. They have ignored how tax havens encourage criminality by offering secrecy to fraudsters, tax cheats and embezzlers, providing the supply-side of the grand corruption that has decimated so many countries.

The failure to tackle these major flaws in the globalized financial system has generated a spirit of lawlessness and unethical behavior that acts as a cancer attacking the integrity of the market system and the democratic ideal. Company directors committed to good governance and ethical policies find themselves competing on an unfair basis against corporate delinquents prepared to push tax avoidance to the limits. Around the world the tax burden is increasingly shifting from the rich to middle-income earners and the less-well-off.

By a process of stealth the global economy has been reconfigured to serve first and foremost the interests of the super-rich. They have become a breed apart, especially in their tax affairs. The majority hold their wealth in offshore tax havens like Jersey, Switzerland or the Cayman Islands. They live more or less where they choose, and their main preoccupation is staying rich. Their assets are mobile, and they can typically decide where and whether to pay tax. Taxes, as property millionaire Leona Helmsley said, are for 'the little people'. When she said this in the 1980s many people were shocked by her remarks. By now things have deteriorated to such an extent that most people expect the rich to avoid paying tax.

For half a century the cancer of tax havens has metastasized through the global economy, causing turmoil, increasing inequality and insecurity, and undermining democracy and national sovereignty. Removing this cancerous growth must now, urgently, be made a global priority.

Thankfully, we detect signs of a global mood shift. US President Barack Obama's Stop Tax Haven Abuse Act was re-submitted to the Senate earlier this year and there are clear signs that many Americans have had enough. Emerging scandals in places like Liechtenstein have hardened attitudes, and the financial crisis has abruptly ended the free-for-all financial deregulation that puffed so much air into the offshore phenomenon. The role of tax havens in catalyzing the global crisis and causing poverty was explicitly recognized by G20 leaders when they met in London in April 2009, causing a flurry of activity in places like Jersey, Austria and Switzerland which were determined to avoid being blacklisted and made subject to international sanctions.

The Tax Justice Network is sounding the alarm, and non-governmental groups are waking up and joining the protests. In March 2009, in the run-up to the G20 Summit, Jersey found itself the unwilling host to demonstrators from across Europe, targeting the island's role as a conduit for flight capital from Majority World countries into the major European capital markets. An epic struggle is now set to emerge, between the super-rich offshore operators and the rest of us.

Returning home to Jersey, I find that dark clouds are gathering. Young islanders cannot afford the high cost of living and are leaving to find jobs elsewhere. Poverty rates are astonishing for an economy with nearly the highest GDP per capita in the world. Jersey's economy now depends almost entirely on its tax haven status, and measures to tackle tax havens will cause major disruption. Jersey people, now learning more about their island's role in impoverishing the world, increasingly feel ashamed.

John Christensen is a development economist who went undercover in Jersey's banking sector to discover how tax havens operate. He also worked as the island's economic adviser from 1987 to 1998. Since leaving Jersey in 1998, he has helped launch the Tax Justice Network and directs its International Secretariat in London.
www.taxjustice.net

Connections: Ann Pettifor, p 21; Susan George, p 49; Peter Stalker, p 97; Nicola Bullard, p 153.

1 Raymond Baker, *Capitalism's Achilles Heel*, John Wiley & Sons, Hoboken, NJ, 2005.
2 Quote from *This Day*, Lagos, Nigeria, 6 June 2005.

126

Rich Get Poorer, Poor Disappear

The 'Nouveau Poor' don't make headlines, but Barbara Ehrenreich argues that any serious attempt to get things going will have to start with them.

Ever on the lookout for the bright side of hard times, I am tempted to delete 'class inequality' from my worry list. Less than a year ago, it was one of the biggest economic threats on the horizon, with even hardline conservative pundits grousing that wealth was flowing uphill at an alarming rate, leaving the middle class stuck with stagnating incomes while the new super-rich ascended to the heavens in their personal jets. Then the whole top-heavy structure of American capitalism began to totter, and – poof! – inequality all but vanished from the public discourse. A financial columnist in the *Chicago Sun Times* has just announced that the recession is a 'great leveler', serving to 'democratize the agony', as we all tumble into 'the Nouveau Poor…'

The media have been pelting us with heart-wrenching stories about the neo-suffering of the Nouveau Poor, or at least the Formerly Super-rich among them: Foreclosures in Greenwich CT! A collapsing market for cosmetic surgery! Sales of Gulfstream jets declining! Niemen Marcus and Saks Fifth Avenue on the ropes! We read of desperate measures, like having to cut back the personal trainer to two hours a week. Parties have been canceled; dinner guests have been offered, gasp, baked potatoes and chili. The *New York Times* relates the story of a New Jersey teenager whose parents were forced to cut her $100-a-week allowance and private Pilates classes. In one of the most pathetic tales of all, New Yorker Alexandra Penney relates how she lost her life savings to Bernie Madoff and is now faced with having to lay off her three-day-a-week maid, Yolanda. 'I wear a classic clean white shirt every day of the week. I have about 40 white shirts. They make me feel fresh and ready to face whatever battles I may be fighting...' she wrote, but without Yolanda, 'how am I going to iron those shirts so I can still feel like a poor civilized person?'

But hard times are no more likely to abolish class inequality than Obama's inauguration is likely to eradicate racism. No-one actually knows yet whether inequality has increased or decreased during the last year of recession, but the historical precedents are not promising. The economists I've talked to – like Biden's top economic advisor, Jared Bernstein – insist that recessions are particularly unkind to the poor and the middle class. Canadian economist Armine Yalnizyan says: 'Income polarization always gets worse during recessions.' It makes sense. If the stock market has shrunk your assets of $500 million to a mere $250 million, you may have to pass on a third or fourth vacation home. But if you've just lost an $8 an hour job, you're looking at no home at all.

All right, I'm a journalist and I understand how the media work. When a millionaire cuts back on his *crème fraîche* and caviar consumption, you have a touching human interest story. But pitch a story about a laid-off roofer who loses his trailer home and you're likely to get a big editorial yawn. 'Poor Get Poorer' is just not an eye-grabbing headline, even when the evidence is overwhelming. Food stamp applications, for example, are rising toward a historic record; calls to one DC-area hunger hotline have jumped 248 per cent in the last six months, most of them from people who have never needed food aid before. And for the first time since 1996, there's been a marked upswing in the number of people seeking cash assistance from TANF (Temporary Aid to Needy Families), the ex-sanguinated version of welfare left by welfare 'reform'. Too bad for them that TANF is essentially a wage-supplement program based on the assumption that the poor would always be able to find jobs, and that it pays, at most, less than half the federal poverty level.

Why do the sufferings of the poor and the downwardly mobile class matter more than the tiny deprivations of the rich? Leaving aside all the soft-hearted socialist, Christian-type arguments, it's because poverty and the squeeze on the middle class are a big part of what got us into this mess in the first place. Only one thing kept the sub-rich spending in the 00s, and hence kept the economy going, and that was debt: credit card debt, home equity loans, car loans, college loans and of course the now famously 'toxic' subprime mortgages, which were bundled and sliced into 'securities' and marketed to the rich as high-interest investments throughout the world. The gross inequality of American society wasn't just unfair or aesthetically displeasing; it created a perilously unstable situation.

Which is why any serious government attempt to get the economy going again – and I leave aside the unserious attempts like bank bailouts and other corporate welfare projects – has to start at the bottom. Obama is promising to generate three million new jobs in 'shovel ready' projects, and let's hope they're not all jobs for young men with strong backs. Until those jobs kick in, and in case they leave out the elderly, the single moms and the downsized desk-workers, we're going to need an economic policy centered on the poor: more money for food stamps, for Medicaid, unemployment insurance, and, yes, cash assistance along the lines of what welfare once was, so that when people come tumbling down they don't end up six feet under. For those who think 'welfare' sounds too radical, we could just call it a 'right to life' program, only one in which the objects of concern have already been born.

If that sounds politically unfeasible, consider this: when Clinton was cutting welfare and food stamps in the 1990s, the poor were still an easily marginalized group, subjected to the nastiest sorts of racial and gender stereotyping. They were lazy, promiscuous, addicted, deadbeats, as whole choruses of conservative experts announced. Thanks to the recession, however – and I knew there had to be a bright side – the ranks of the poor are swelling every day with failed business owners, office workers, salespeople and long-time homeowners. Stereotype that! As the poor and the formerly middle-class Nouveau Poor become the American majority, they will finally have the clout to get their needs met.

Barbara Ehrenreich is the author of 13 books, including the *New York Times* bestseller *Nickel and Dimed*. A frequent contributor to the *New York Times, Harpers,* and the *Progressive*, she is a contributing writer to *Time* magazine. She lives in Florida.

This is reprinted, with permission, from her blog http://ehrenreich.blogs.com/

Connections: Noam Chomsky, p 33; Naomi Klein, p 45; Yash Tandon p 131; Richard Wilkinson & Kate Pickett, p 143.

Jobs First

Yash Tandon puts jobs, trade and finance in their proper places.

Capitalism has been in crisis many times since Adam Smith wrote his famous theoretical treatise rationalizing it 260 years ago. It has always managed to re-emerge – though sometimes severely bruised. As a global system, it is adept at reviving and reinventing itself. The dominant economic classes – currently the global corporations – have always succeeded in getting whoever is in state power to serve their ends. This has been true whether the political leaders come from conservative, democratic, or social democratic backgrounds; whether they are members of the aristocracy or the working class.

Meanwhile, the conditions of the working peoples of the world have only marginally improved. They have reaped some of the benefits of progress overall, yes, but their condition has not improved as much as it should given the extraordinary developments of science, technology and the organization of production and distribution. Indeed, the plight of vast numbers of people, especially in the southern hemisphere, may well have deteriorated – in terms of their habitat, the quality of food they consume, their access to health, education, energy and other basic amenities of life.

The current crisis raises some new questions. For example, is this crisis qualitatively different from all previous ones? Has speculative, financialized capital – based not on real values but on fictitious bubbles – so transformed the nature of capitalism that it is now far less able to recover?

It also raises questions about the G20 – a group that is fast complementing, possibly replacing, the G8 – and its leaders. Some G20 leaders do not have their origins in the privileged classes. Could they make any major difference to the evolution of capitalism in our times? President Lula of Brazil, born into a working-class family, worked as a lathe operator in a factory. Barack Obama was born into a humble, mixed African and American background, and rose from the periphery of the US political-financial system to become President of the world's most capitalist country. Does the fact that these two key G20 leaders do not come from the heart of finance capital make them more open to transforming the global system to make it more favorable to the working peoples of the world?

The question is crucial because the world faces massive job losses triggered by the crisis, not just in the financial sector but in the real economy. Figures for rising unemployment vary, but in China alone we are looking at 25 million job cuts in the current year. Globally, according to the International Labour Organization (ILO), the figures could run to 50 or 100 million. The world has witnessed 'jobless growth' in the past. But what we are witnessing today is an unparalleled shrinking of jobs on a global scale.

The root of the crisis lies in one of globalization's most flawed pieces of logic: the privileging of trade over industry, of finance over production. Symptomatically, the Geneva-based World Trade Organization (WTO) has grabbed the global and media spotlight to a far greater extent than the United Nations

Industry and Development Organization (UNIDO). It should have been the other way round. Industry precedes trade; if there is no production there is no trade. One of the more hopeful possible side-effects of the current failure of the Doha Round of Trade negotiations is that governments and their advisors might begin to prioritize production and industrialization over trade.

For sure, a development-friendly outcome of the Doha Round would have been a good thing. But the fact that it has gone into a stalemate is indicative of a deeper malaise in the system. That it should come at the same time as the collapse of the global financial system is no accident. The simultaneous near-death, or at least ill-legitimization, of both the WTO and the Bretton Woods institutions (the World Bank and the International Monetary Fund) is related to a dual weakness in the global economic system – the dominance of trade over industry, and of finance over production.

Of the two, the latter is the more serious problem. Financialization of production has put a premium on speculative profits, often made out of fictitious money or credit, rather than where the emphasis should be – on production itself. Ponzi schemes (fraudulent investment operations that pay returns to investors out of the money paid by subsequent investors rather than from profit) of the kind run by Bernard Madoff duped millions into believing that they were putting their investments into the real economy, whereas they were only putting them into a deep black hole. Even reputable banks, mostly in the Western world, were fooled.

As for trade, trading in money constitutes almost 98 per cent of all financial transactions; only 2 per cent or less actually finance trade in real goods. This is the topsy-turvy world in which we live. The present global system's trading and financing architecture has serious defects that render the system exposed to manipulation by crooks and cranks.

This is not to underestimate the importance of either finance or trade. What is produced must be financed and traded, of course. However, finance is, or should be, only a means to production, and not a means to self-accumulation without production (money turned into more money in the 'money market'), as is the case in the current phase of financialized capitalism.

It is important to remember that there are at least three other ingredients to production – labor power, natural resources and entrepreneurial skills. In the present global system of production, banks and entrepreneurs are inordinately privileged over labor and natural resources. A chief executive officer (CEO) of a big transnational can earn a salary of over a million dollars a month, whereas a worker gets a tiny fraction of that, especially if he or she (especially she) is located in the countries of the Global South. That is one of the fundamental underlying reasons why rich countries become richer and poor countries stay poor.

Trade is important. After goods are produced they must be consumed. Of course, not all that is produced is necessarily traded; subsistence farmers in much of the South, for example, consume what they produce without going through the market. Nonetheless, markets are important for distribution of goods produced, and for realizing the value contained in the goods so that the production cycle begins again.

However, the global trading system is heavily loaded against the countries of the South for both historical and structural reasons. The natural resources of the South are seriously undervalued in the global market. If you factor in the real value of the labor power of the workers of the South, and add the environmental cost of exploitation of the South's resources, then the countries in the South should be getting at least four or five times more value than they currently receive.

Even when it comes to production, there is an anomaly in the system. Apart from the undervaluation of labor power and natural resources of the South, the combination of factors of production is heavily weighted in favor of the suppliers of capital and patented technology. And there is very little 'transfer of technology'.

A study carried out by the United Nations Conference on Trade and Development (UNCTAD) in 2007 on the Least Developed Countries (LDCs) found that most have opened up their economies to global trade and are highly integrated in the global economy, but they are not climbing the economic and technological ladder.

The study covered 11 LDCs over a two-year period (2004-06) including six African, four Asian and one Caribbean. It showed that the LDCs continue to import high-value machinery and equipment which are paid out of low-value exports in the production chain and a long-term decline in the terms of trade. Domestic firms and farms in LDCs have low technology capabilities.

Out of the 24 value chains of LDC exports, upgrading had occurred in only 9 since the 1990s, and downgrading in 12, representing 52 per cent of LDC exports. The study of 155 firms in Bangladesh, for example, showed that there was no development of technological capacity in agro-processing, textiles, garments or pharmaceuticals. As for the much-touted myth that foreign direct investments (FDIs) are a means to transferring technological knowhow, the study found that the FDIs have not helped LDCs much.

The problem is not lack of openness to foreign investors, but rather the quality of integration of transnational corporations (TNCs) into host countries' economies. Most FDIs concentrated on mineral extraction in enclaves with little spillover into the domestic economy.

The UNCTAD study put this all down to 'economic liberalization without learning', global integration without innovation. This resulted in the increasing marginalization of 767 million people in the LDCs. These countries are locked into low value-added commodity production and low-skill manufacturing. This is in sharp contrast to the East Asian countries such as Japan, Korea and Taiwan, which encouraged technological learning during their early phase of industrialization.

Let us take the case of Africa. In the past 30 years the free trade dogma enforced by the IMF and the World Bank as part of their lending conditionalities has brought about industrial havoc in Africa. Forced tariff reductions opened up African economies to highly competitive (and, in the case of imports from Europe, highly subsidized) products that devastated African industries. In Uganda and Tanzania, for example, the many textile manufacturing enterprises – which had created jobs and developed the domestic and regional markets in the wake of their independence from colonial rule – became hostage to tariff reductions and were mostly gone by the 1990s. The countries became dependent on imports of clothing. In the mania to export all that is best, Ugandans exported their best stock of fish, leaving people, including fisherfolk, to eat fish bones, to which poor people have given the exalted name of 'fillet'. Africa has become a net importer of food and manufactured products, creating in its wake massive unemployment in the formal sector and conditions for the export of labor (including skilled labor) mostly to developed countries.

What should developing countries do? One important lesson to draw from history and the current phase of capitalist globalization is that developing countries must have policy space in order to design their economic roadmap. This is what is seriously compromised in the dogmatic pursuit of neoliberal globalization. Market fundamentalism has replaced common sense. Now, in the wake of the financial crisis, common sense must return – production must be privileged over trade and jobs over finance.

In the case of Africa, for example, for 30 years it was assumed that the best experts came from outside the continent, from institutions such as the World Bank, the International Monetary Fund, the Organization for Economic Co-operation and Development (OECD). These so-called experts have fallen flat on their faces. Africa and the rest of the developing world must now seize this opportunity to take matters in their own hands – to restore their devastated economies by using their own human and natural resources.

The G20 Summit came and went in early April 2009. As expected by those who can differentiate between hype and reality, it achieved very little.

To the question raised earlier – whether political leaders not from the heart of finance capital are more open to transforming the global system in favor of the working peoples of the world – the answer seems to be 'no'. Judging by the Declaration of the G20 they are not capable of making any fundamental change in the system. This has nothing to do with their class origins. It has more to do with the nature of the global and state system they are serving. Short of groundswell pressure from below for a radical break with the past, the current leaders of the G20 will at best only tinker with the system.

Thus, instead of directly helping out ordinary people and job-creating small enterprises, the G20 put all their bailout money into the very banks that are at the root of the financial crisis. Even then, the highly inflated and publicized figure of $1.1 trillion turns out to be largely recycled money. The biggest benefactor is the IMF, with a large boost of $500 billion. However, and this is important, while the G20 has called upon the IMF to review its lending conditionalities to ensure that borrowing countries adopt 'counter-cyclical' measures, the reality – as the examples of its lending to Pakistan and several East European countries show – is that the IMF has made no change in its loan conditions. These countries are expected to follow pro-cyclical measures, including fiscal and monetary policy tightening. Furthermore, while the G20 talked about keeping 'an open global economy', in reality practically all of them (especially the US) have put in place measures to protect their industries and jobs even as they demand that others open their doors to liberalized trade. There is thinly disguised hypocrisy in the G20 leaders' public international posturing and action at the state and country level.

In these circumstances, what should developing countries do? In the immediate to short term, they should do at least the following:

- Put a moratorium on payment of all debts they owe to both bilateral and multilateral 'donors'. This is not to dishonor the debts but to buy time to study the nature of these debts and to separate those that are legitimate and those that are not.

- Review all the donor agreements (for example, those with the IMF, the World Bank, USAID and the European Commission), in order to remove from them offending conditions that compromise their policy options. The review should be carried out by a process that involves all stakeholders – government, the civil society, the trade unions, and the private sector – without the presence of the so-called experts from the North.

- Establish regional commissions to look into further steps towards regional integration, focusing on creating regional banks, regional reserve funds, a regional currency, and regional steps that might be immediately put in place to safeguard local and regional manufacturing, agriculture, services (such as health, energy and water), and food security.

- Provide appropriate incentives and backup support in order to create national and regional markets and jobs for the people. These measures could include seasonal credit for agriculture; storage, marketing, pricing and last-resort purchasing facilities for agricultural produce; tariff protection for local industries and manufacturing; banking and financial services for productive enterprises so that people's savings are channeled to these enterprises rather than externalized in Western banks and tax havens; proper wages for workers and professional-sector employees so that instead of migrating they stay at home and provide these necessary services.

- Create institutional structures to promote the development of science and technology, and encourage innovation in areas ranging from food production to mining and manufacturing and health and welfare facilities. Knowledge is the key to global production and competition. The trend of economic globalization is increasingly towards the development of intellectual rather than physical assets. It is here that most developing countries (and not only the LDCs) are still hostage to the monopolization of knowledge. The knowledge divide between rich and poor nations has increased, especially over the last three decades of globalization. The current intellectual property (IP) regimes lock out patented technologies from the reach of developing countries. These countries must provide the necessary incentives and structures to encourage the harnessing, documenting, registering and disseminating of local knowledge, and must build their industrial and agricultural capacity based on this knowledge, while not closing the option to borrow or purchase from outside what cannot be produced at home.

All this is not to ignore the highly controversial debate on technology transfer with regard to climate change. The world has to move towards a low-carbon economy. But how to do this is a challenge. Much depends on the transfer of technology for emission reduction and adaptation from the North to the South. The North would want to define this as part of Official Development Assistance. But it should not be. It is part of the commitment that the rich countries have made to the poor countries in the United Nations Framework Convention on Climate Change. The bigger problem, however, is not money or even technology. The bigger problem is the IP content of the technology, because through it the corporations of the North that have the technologies would use the IP regimes to control the processes necessary for emission control and adaptation.

At the heart of technology is innovation, and at the heart of innovation is the economics of knowledge production and dissemination. The Northern governments, aided and abetted by their corporations, have created a formidable array of national and international structures such as Anti-Counterfeit Trade Agreement, Global IP Center, the International Medicinal Products Anti-Counterfeit Taskforce (IMPACT), and Standards Employed by Customs for Uniform Rights Enforcement (SECURE). The North has smuggled some of these into the body fabric of intergovernmental organizations, for example, SECURE within the World Customs Organization and IMPACT within the World Health Organization. The resultant multi-headed monster breathes more fire and generates more heat than the mythical Chinese dragon.

Putting industry above trade, and prioritizing production over bailing out the banks, are imperative for development and creating employment. Trade and finance are, of course, important, but they are the means and not the end. The global political class that constitutes the G20 is unlikely to pick up the challenge thrown at them by the world's working peoples in the farms, factories and fishing grounds of production. Whatever their class or social origins, they are, by and large, serving the interest of the ruling global financial oligarchy. If, in the process, they create some jobs and placate the rising tide of discontent seething from below, they will have, from their point of view, fulfilled their mission.

Citizen movements all over the world – including trade unions, peasant and farmer co-operatives, women and youth groups, human rights, environmental, activist and student movements – have an obligation to take up the gauntlet. They might reflect and act on a two-track strategy. The first track is to continue working with the people at the grassroots and networking with one another, and to encourage and support all ideas and activities offering alternatives to the current dominant model of organizing production, trade and resource distribution. The second is to continue to demand of the political leadership in their countries that they seriously address issues of job security, food security, and the provision of the basic needs of the majority of the world's people, even if such leaders are incapable of meeting these demands.

There is an African anecdote that is worth remembering. A young guitar player was asked by his audience to play again and again – once more, *encore*, they demanded. Feeling flattered, the guitarist begged: 'Please let me stop here; I am overwhelmed by your appreciation of my music.' In response, one of the members of the audience replied on behalf of the rest: 'No, you must go on again and again, and we shall not rest, until you get it right.'

Citizen movements the world over must continue making their demands on their political leadership 'until they get it right' – or until they are replaced by those who understand and can deliver what the people demand.

Ugandan-born **Yash Tandon** is the former Executive Director of the South Centre. He is currently Chair of the Southern and Eastern African Trade Information and Negotiations Institute (SEATINI).

Connections: Walden Bello, p 57; Peter Stalker, p 97; John Hilary, p 217.

SUSAN
FORGE
NAOMI
KLEIN
CHOMSKY
NOAM
ANN
PETTIFOR
DAVID
RANSOM
JOHN
HILARY
PAT
BOND

DANNY RIVERS
DEREK WALL
MICHAEL ALBERT
EVO MORALES
NICOLA BULLARD
RICHARD WILKINSON & KATE PICKETT

Equality Is Better – For Everyone

Few people have looked as long at the hard evidence as **Richard Wilkinson** and **Kate Pickett**. Their new book, *The Spirit Level*, shows the terrible toll inequality takes not just on the poor, but on entire societies. As a result, political movements that aim for greater equality can do a great deal of good.

We have got close to the end of what economic growth can do for us. For thousands of years the best way of improving the quality of human life was to raise material living standards. When the wolf was never far from the door, good times were simply times of plenty. But for the vast majority of people in affluent countries the difficulties of life are no longer about filling our stomachs, having clean water and keeping warm. Today, not only have measures of wellbeing and happiness ceased to rise with economic growth but, as affluent societies have grown richer, there have been long-term rises in rates of anxiety, depression and numerous other social problems. The populations of rich countries have got to the end of a long historical journey.

Among poorer countries, life expectancy increases rapidly during the early stages of economic development – then the rate of improvement slows down. As living standards continue to rise and countries get richer and richer, the relationship between economic growth and life expectancy weakens. Eventually it disappears entirely, as has already happened in the richest 30 or so countries.

This is not because we have reached the limits of life expectancy. Even the richest countries go on enjoying substantial improvements in health as time goes by. What has changed is that the improvements have ceased to be related to average living standards. With every ten years that pass, life expectancy in rich countries increases by between two and three years. This happens regardless of economic growth, so that a country as rich as the US no longer does better than Greece or New Zealand, although they are not much more than half as rich. Looking at the data, we cannot help but conclude that as countries get richer, further increases in average living standards do less and less for health and wellbeing.

Whether we look at health, happiness or other measures of wellbeing, there is a consistent picture. In poorer countries, economic development continues to be very important for human wellbeing. Increases in material living standards result in substantial improvements both in objective measures of wellbeing, like life expectancy, and in subjective ones, like happiness. But as nations join the ranks of the affluent, further rises in income count for less and less.

In affluent countries, we are the first generation to have to find new answers to the question of how we can make further improvements to the real quality of human life. What should we turn to if not to economic growth? One of the most powerful clues comes from the fact that we are affected very differently by income differences *within our own society* from the way we are affected by the differences in average income *between one rich society and another.*

A series of health and social problems like violence, mental illness, teenage births and educational failure are all more common among poorer people within rich countries. As a result, it often looks as if the effects of higher incomes and living standards are to lift people out of these problems. But when we make comparisons between different societies, we find that these problems have little or no relation to levels of *average* incomes between different countries. Richer people tend, on average, to be healthier and happier than poorer people in the same society. But, comparing rich countries, it makes no difference whether, on average, people in one society are almost twice as rich as people in another. How can we explain this apparent paradox?

Some people might think the pattern is created by the most vulnerable and least healthy people moving down the social hierarchy. Others think that these problems concentrate in deprived areas because of lower material standards of living – poor housing and diets, for example. Some think that intelligence or genetic factors are the explanation. But, increasingly, it is apparent that it is low social status itself, or low relative income compared to others in the same society, that is the problem.

Among the rich market economies of the world, there are stark differences in income inequality. Among the more equal societies are the Nordic countries and Japan, where the incomes of the top 20 per cent are three or four times as big as the incomes of the poorest 20 per cent. Among the more unequal societies are countries like the US, Portugal and Britain, where the richest 20 per cent are eight or nine times as rich as the poorest 20 per cent. It looks as if the problems associated with deprivation within a country all become more frequent as material differences increase.

In societies where income differences between rich and poor are smaller, the statistics show that community life is stronger and levels of trust are higher. There is also less violence, including lower homicide rates; physical and mental health tends to be better and life expectancy is higher. In fact, most of the problems related to relative deprivation are reduced: prison populations are smaller, teenage birth rates are lower, educational scores tend to be higher, there is less obesity and more social mobility.

What is surprising is how big these differences are. Mental illness is three times more common in more unequal countries than in the most equal, obesity rates are twice as high, rates of imprisonment eight times higher, and teenage births increase tenfold.

If health and social problems are concentrated among the most deprived because the vulnerable and unhealthy drift down the social scale, this doesn't explain why they are so much more frequent in more unequal countries. Similarly, the relationship can't be explained in terms of any fixed factor, such as genetics, because levels of these problems change over time – think of the current obesity epidemic or the rise in imprisonment. And if these problems were simply the result of low material living standards, they would diminish with economic growth. Instead, what seems to matter is the scale of social class differentiation and inequality in any society.

In our book, we test these patterns in two separate test-beds, not only among the rich, developed countries, but also in comparisons of the 50 US states. The picture that emerges is almost identical in both settings. Our findings confirm the widely held intuition that inequality is socially corrosive.

And just as health inequalities are not simply differences between the health of the poor and everybody else, but instead form a gradient all the way up the social ladder, so that even those near the top do worse than those just above them, so the impact of inequality is not confined to the poor. Indeed, you cannot explain the very large differences we find in rates of health and social problems between more equal and less equal societies by what is happening among the poor. The differences are big because almost everybody is affected.

Where the data allow us to compare people at a given level of income or education or social class between one society and another, it is clear that even the well-off do better in more equal countries. Even well-educated people with good incomes will be likely to live longer and enjoy better health, and their children will do better in school, will be less likely to take drugs and less likely to become teenage parents. Everyone enjoys the benefits of living in a more trusting, less violent society. And although the benefits of greater equality are larger lower down the social scale, they are still apparent high up the social ladder.

The reason why almost everyone benefits from greater equality is that more equal societies are more collaborative, with less status competition. With bigger material inequalities, people become more worried about how they are seen and judged, more vulnerable to status anxieties. So much so, that more unequal societies become more consumerist – people work longer hours, save less of their income and are more likely to get into debt. Greater sensitivity to how we are valued or respected explains why violence is more common in more unequal societies. Disrespect, humiliation and loss of face are common triggers to violence. Perhaps the reason why rates of mental illness are so much higher in more unequal countries is because the quality of social relationships and feeling valued have always been crucial to human wellbeing.

Other human beings have the capacity to be our most feared rivals or our greatest source of support, co-operation and security. We have evolved to be very sensitive to the quality of social relationships. Status matters but so does friendship among equals. Material inequalities play a crucial role in putting barriers between us. When these differences are larger, the balance shifts from us trusting other people and viewing them as friends, to mistrust and competition for status.

Focusing attention on inequalities within affluent societies does not mean ignoring the international inequalities between rich and poor countries. The evidence strongly suggests that narrowing income differences within rich countries makes them more responsive to the needs of poorer countries. More equal societies don't just function better internally; the effects seem to carry over into their external relations. More equal countries give more in foreign aid and score better on the Global Peace Index. They recycle a higher proportion of their waste and think it more important to abide by international environmental agreements.

Politics was once seen as a way of improving people's social and emotional wellbeing by changing their economic circumstances, but over the last few decades the bigger picture has been lost. However, it is now clear that income distribution provides policy-makers with a way of improving the psychosocial wellbeing of whole populations. Politicians have an opportunity to do genuine good. What is essential, if we are to bring a better society into being, is to develop a sustained movement committed to doing that. Policy changes will need to be consistently devoted to this end over several decades – and that requires a society which knows where it wants to go.

The initial task is to gain a widespread public understanding of what is at stake. Rather than allowing this to be just one more idea that briefly gains attention before fashionable opinion moves on, we need to build a social movement committed to its realization. It must be taken up and pursued by a network of shared ideas and action everywhere, in homes and offices, in trade unions and political parties, in churches and schools. It needs also to be pursued by the pressure groups, charities and services concerned. And this needs to be coupled with the urgent task of dealing with global warming. In all these settings we must speak out and explain the advantages of a more equal society.

We should not allow ourselves to be cowed by the idea that higher taxes on the rich will lead to their mass emigration and economic catastrophe. We know that more egalitarian countries live well, with high living standards and much better social environments. We know also that economic growth is not the yardstick by which everything else must be judged. Indeed, we know that it no longer contributes to the real quality of our lives and that consumerism is a danger to the planet.

Nor should we allow ourselves to believe that the rich are scarce and precious members of a superior race of more intelligent beings on whom the rest of us are dependent. That is merely the illusion that wealth and power create. Rather than adopting an attitude of gratitude towards the rich, we need to recognize what a damaging effect they have on the social fabric.

The current economic crisis shows us how dangerous huge salaries and bonuses at the top can be. As well as leading those in charge of our financial institutions to adopt policies that put the wellbeing of whole populations in jeopardy, the very existence of the super-rich increased the pressure to consume, as everyone tried to keep up. The long speculative boom that preceded the financial crash was fueled substantially by the growth of consumers' expenditure. Increased inequality led people to reduce their savings, increase their bank overdrafts and credit card debt, and arrange second mortgages to fund consumption. By adding to the speculative element in the cycles of economic boom and bust, great inequality shifts our attention from pressing environmental and social problems and makes us worry about unemployment, insecurity and 'how to get the economy moving again'.

If the US were to reduce its income inequality to something like the average of the four most equal of the rich countries (Japan, Norway, Sweden and Finland), the proportion of the population feeling they could trust others might rise by 75 per cent; rates of mental illness and obesity might similarly each be cut by almost two-thirds; teenage birth rates could be more than halved; prison populations might be reduced by three-quarters; and people could live longer while working the equivalent of two months less per year. Similarly, Britain could see levels of trust rise to as high as two-thirds against what they are now; mental illness might be more than halved; everyone would get an additional year of life; teenage birth rates could fall to one-third of what they are now; homicide rates could fall by 75 per cent; and everyone could get the equivalent of almost seven weeks extra holiday a year. Reducing inequality would not only make the quality of life better and the economic system more stable, it could also make a major contribution to environmental sustainability.

Over the next generation or so, politics seem likely to be dominated either by efforts to prevent runaway global warming or, if they fail, by attempts to deal with its consequences. How might greater equality and policies to reduce emissions go together? Given what inequality does to a society, and particularly how it heightens competitive consumption, it looks not only as if the two are complementary, but also as if governments may be unable to make big enough cuts in carbon emissions without also reducing inequality.

Rather than assuming that we are stuck with levels of self-interested consumerism, individualism and materialism that must defeat any attempts to develop sustainable economic systems, we need to recognize that these are not fixed expressions of human nature. Instead, they reflect the characteristics of the societies in which we find ourselves and vary even from one rich country to another. At the most fundamental level, reducing inequality is about shifting the balance from the divisive, self-interested consumerism driven by status competition, towards a more socially integrated and affiliative society.

Modern societies will depend increasingly on being creative, adaptable, inventive, well-informed and flexible communities, able to respond generously to each other and to needs wherever they arise. Those are characteristics not of societies in hock to the rich, in which people are driven by status insecurities, but of populations used to working together and respecting each other as equals. And, because we are trying to grow the new society within the old, our values and the way we work must be part of how we bring a new society into being. But we must also try to bring about a shift in public values so that instead of inspiring admiration and envy, conspicuous consumption is seen as part of the problem, a sign of greed and unfairness which damages society and the planet.

At this stage, creating the political will to make society more equal is more important than pinning our colors to a particular set of policies to reduce inequality. Political will depends on the development of a vision of a better society that is both achievable and inspiring. After several decades in which we have lived with the oppressive sense that there is no alternative to the social and environmental failure of modern societies, we now have a chance to regain the sense of optimism which comes from knowing that problems can be solved. It falls to our generation to make one of the biggest transformations in human history. There is a better society to be won.

Richard Wilkinson is Professor Emeritus at the University of Nottingham Medical School and Honorary Professor at University College London.

Kate Pickett is a Senior Lecturer at the University of York and a National Institute for Health Research Career Scientist.

This is an edited extract taken, with permission, from their book *The Spirit Level: Why More Equal Societies Almost Always Do Better*, published in most countries by Penguin and in the US by Bloomsbury.

Connections: Barbara Ehrenreich, p 127; Nicola Bullard, p 153; Evo Morales, p 165; Michael Albert, p 169; Derek Wall, p 181.

WALDEN
BELLO
SUSAN
GEORGE
NAOMI
KLEIN
NOAM
CHOMSKY
ANN
PETTIFOR
DAVID
RANSOM

To Live Well

Nicola Bullard waves goodbye to macho economics and outlines alternatives for a more democratic, greener, more female-friendly future.

These days, everything is in 'crisis', whether it's the financial crisis, economic crisis, credit crisis, food crisis, climate crisis, or the catch-all global crisis. In the first three months of 2009, *The Financial Times* used the word 6,465 times. Like 'terror' in the Bush era, crisis has become the word that defines the moment. And like 'terror' it is used in such a de-contextualized way and from such a Western-centric perspective, that it glosses over the deeper causes of the crises and the connections between them.

But most of all, it ignores the bitter fact that the Majority World lives daily in a state of crisis. It is only when food prices sky-rocket in the urban centers or the financial markets crash in Wall Street or the City of London that the global élite sits up and takes note.

But while they happily throw billions, even trillions, of our money at their 'crisis' they seem unable to join the dots and see the line that connects all these eruptions.

The crisis is real enough, but it is not simply the result of overproduction or underconsumption or bad lending or even lack of regulation; it is a profound crisis of social and ecological reproduction.[1]

Although you will never read it in the newspapers, theologians, feminists and Marxists all agree: capitalism destroys nature and alienates society, and the no-holds-barred free-market capitalism of the past 30 years, in particular, has been terrifyingly effective at both.

As Marxist ecologist John Bellamy Foster explains: 'What made this new system [capitalism] work was the incessant accumulation of capital in one cycle after another, with each new phase of accumulation taking the last as its starting point. This meant ever more divided, more alienated human beings, together with a more globally destructive metabolism between humanity and nature.'[2]

The late feminist philosopher, Teresa Brennan, also talks about the destructive character of capitalism: 'In the short run, profit is made by consuming the sources of long-run profit (nature and labor) faster than they can adequately reproduce themselves – or, to say the same thing, faster than the time it takes to meet human needs or safeguard the environment.'[3]

And economist Ulrich Duchrow and theologian Franz Hinkelammert argue that the sole goal of globalization – the most voracious version of capitalism seen so far – is to liberate the 'accumulation of capital from all social and ecological barriers. The result is the total market, which is in the process not just of destroying life on earth but with it its own foundations'.[4]

So while financial capitalism is *attacking* nature and society, the main objective of the G20 (the exclusive group of the most powerful economies in the world) is to put it back on its feet, kick-start the financial engines, and get economies growing again. But growth is the problem or, at least, the kind of economic growth that depends on devouring society and nature at a speed and intensity that outstrip their respective capacities to regenerate and reproduce.

In the logic of ever-expanding globalization, when nature is depleted in one location, capital – for example, logging or mining or steel production – simply moves to another location. When labor becomes too expensive in one country, factories relocate to where the wages are lower, or when populations get too old to look after their elders or their children, they import cheap (young and usually female) labor in the form of migration. The suburbs of Rome, Los Angeles or Beirut are filled with Filipinas who have left their own children in villages on the other side of the earth, to care for the ageing parents of middle-class workers who themselves face the same prospect. All this results from the pursuit of profit that has, as Duchrow and Hinkelammert note, become completely de-linked from the constraints or limits of society and nature. These links were first severed in Britain during the industrial revolution of the 18th century and the dissociation between product and producer, between nature and society, has become more abstract and attenuated ever since, as production chains extend across the globe, capturing and transforming into profit the labor and natural resources of societies and ecosystems far removed from the point of consumption. This form of economic production works hand in hand with a particular form of social reproduction called patriarchy, which is essentially the institutionalized inequality between men and women, which no amount of free market consumer choice can obliterate, despite the advertising.

So, the situation is bad and we need to do a lot of things. As a start, I suggest three really big things that we need to do to make life a whole lot better for nearly everyone, and especially women, and maybe a bit worse for the extremely rich and greedy (mainly men). Here's the short version:

First, we need to expand the common good. Second, we need to cool the planet. And third, we need to share our common wealth.

Expanding the common good

What is the common good? Duckrow and Hinkelammert offer a simple starting point, which is ethical, humane and just: '...the perspective of the common good fundamentally starts with the weakest, most threatened members of the community. If they can live, all can live.'[5] This means, obviously, children, the sick and disabled, unemployed, elderly. But, if we take a global vision of 'community', it also means landless farmers, indigenous peoples, the urban poor, underpaid and precarious workers, women in many situations, people of color and migrants. The list is long, and it adds up to the majority of humanity. The environment, too, is a common good – surely the ultimate common good because it contains the source of life itself – and its protection is paramount.

From this ethical (and pragmatic) basis – ensuring that the weakest can live and that the environment is protected for future generations – it is imperative that we save society and nature from the logic of profit and expand the commons.

Water, land, food, health, education, social security and pensions, public transport, housing, hospitals and schools, seeds, culture, knowledge and even democracy itself, must be de-commodified, taken out of the market, and extended to all people, in all societies.

Internet, information and communications, similarly, should be available to all. There should be free wi-fi, computer centers in thousands of (new and old) public libraries, and mobile phones in everyone's hands: we are humans, we love to talk to each other, and the richness of exchange, encounter, learning, creating and sharing that is possible because of information technology is one of the great advances of our age (noting, of course, that we also need to deal with the environmental impact of throw-away computer technology). 'Open-source' is a radical movement challenging capitalist property rights, and it should be extended to many more fields, including one of the bastions of intellectual property rights protection, the pharmaceutical industry.

Expanding the commons should be possible – it is an ethical not an economic question. It is also a political strategy: to reduce the spaces controlled by corporations, institutions, brands and consumerism, and to expand the spaces for sharing the 'common good'. The commons does not have to be controlled by the State, indeed there are many common goods that can and should be managed by communities, by those who produce and use the goods, collectively and democratically, or even by individual actions in the spirit of gift and counter-gift. But perhaps most of all, it could be an emancipatory strategy for creating new possibilities of participation and control by those who have been excluded from power.

Cooling the planet

We are dumping too much carbon dioxide and other 'greenhouse' gases into the atmosphere. This makes the earth heat up, which in turn disrupts our climate and weather systems, causing floods and droughts and heat waves and storms that, more often than not, strike the people with the least resources to protect themselves. The vast majority of these gases come from the fossil fuels that drive the expansion of global capitalism, providing the energy to make and move all the stuff that we consume and throw away.

So we have to stop pumping greenhouse gases into the atmosphere, which means we need to reduce our use of fossil fuels. But we also need to regenerate ecosystems that have been destroyed, usually in the pursuit of profit.

There are many other things that should be done, now. For a start, the industrial model of agriculture is a major contributor to greenhouse gas emissions: if we shifted to organic agriculture, shortened the distance between production and consumption (food miles) and guaranteed land to peasant farmers, it would go a long way to reducing emissions and stopping the environmental devastation that results from land-grabbing and large-scale industrial agriculture.

For the international peasants' movement, La Via Campesina, this alternative model of agriculture is 'food sovereignty':

'Food sovereignty is the right of peoples to healthy and culturally-appropriate food produced through ecologically sound and sustainable methods, and their right to define their own food and agriculture systems. It puts the aspirations and needs of those who produce, distribute and consume food at the heart of food systems and policies rather than the demands of markets and corporations.'[6]

Like industrial agriculture, agro-fuels are an environmental disaster, displacing food production and sucking up massive amounts of water. Industrial-scale agro-fuel production should also be banned.

Deforestation is a source of carbon dioxide, and reforestation is important. But this should not be done through the market: it makes no sense for polluting industries to buy 'carbon credits' in the financial market based on some notional 'carbon capture' in a forest in Brazil. For a start, why should the financial markets make even more money when they already owe us (big time) for bailing them out of this financial mess? Second, it would be much simpler if the polluting industry just cut its pollution. Then the people who live near the factory would be better off and forest regeneration would not depend on pollution somewhere else. What's more, most of the forest destruction happens because of the demand for wood and paper (causing the destruction of biodiverse forests which are replaced by monoculture plantations), and the encroachment of industrial agriculture and agro-fuels into forests. Taking care of our biodiversity and forests is part of the common good, but it will also help cool the planet.

Cities, too, are important. More than half the world's population is now urbanized, living in what David Harvey calls 'divided and conflict-prone' cities.[7] Class relations, he says, are 'etched on the spatial forms of our cities, which increasingly consist of fortified fragments, gated communities and privatized public spaces kept under constant surveillance.' He could also have noted that gender relations are etched in the city, not only in terms of the spaces available to women, but the violence that makes many cities so unsafe for women of all ages. Reclaiming and de-privatizing space, transport, housing and culture are important. But reclaiming the city as a common good, and re-appropriating the wealth created by the city for the common good is vital. Reconfiguring the geography of cities, and especially transforming the energy-intensive lifestyle of the suburbs, to create low-carbon, women-friendly, diverse and people-powered cities is one of the most exciting opportunities of our times.

Sharing the wealth

As we have seen in the last months, there is a lot of money going around. This money is being used to prop up a financial and economic system that is fundamentally unfair and unsustainable, yet governments hand it over to the banks with almost no strings attached. At the same time, 30 years of free-market indoctrination has left most countries and most people thinking that it is not possible to expand the commons, or fund public services, to provide decent health and pension systems, or even to raise wages. But in both the North and the South, the rich are getting richer and paying a lot less tax.

A recent report from the Institute of Policy Studies shows that America's top 400 taxpayers in 1955 paid three times more of their income in taxes than the top 400 of 2006, the most recent year with data available. IPS calculates that if the most affluent 400 of 2006 had paid as much of their incomes in taxes as the top 400 in 1955, the US Federal Treasury would have collected $35.9 billion more revenue in 2006 just from these 400 ultra-rich individuals.[8]

Although the trend is not as dramatic in other industrialized countries, in much of the South tax revenue is mainly from indirect sources such as value added taxes (VAT), a state of affairs that is very good for the rich and very bad for the poor. It also leaves the State with a narrow revenue base, which increases its dependence on private sector investment, external loans and aid, and reduces the capacity for expanding the commons and redistribution. Progressive tax reform is imperative in the South and the North, as well as closing all tax havens and ensuring that corporations pay their fair share.

Apart from a decent progressive tax base, there are other sources of revenue for financing the expanded commons and cooling the planet: military expenditure in almost every country is both too high and too secretive. Demilitarization is one obvious way of increasing budget allocations to the common good.

Another striking characteristic of this era of capitalism is that the share of profits between labor and capital is the worst it has ever been. Raising workers' wages is essential as a starting point for redistributing wealth, and it is also true that higher wages are an incentive for better investment in health, education and safe working conditions. Well-paid and well-organized (women and men) workers are less 'disposable' than those who are precarious and exploited. This of course presumes a major shift in the current correlation of forces between labor and capital. However, if labor could engage in this struggle with a broader vision of expanding the welfare and common good of all, rather than a small élite of organized workers, then the balance of forces could change.

Someone has to pay the costs of surviving climate chaos and transitioning to low-carbon economies. According to the UN Framework Convention on Climate Change, the industrialized countries that have the historical responsibility for greenhouse gas emissions also have a binding responsibility to act, both in terms of finance and technology. But the concept of 'ecological debt' goes one step further, and captures many of the ethical problems in the historical relationship between North and South, and between capitalism, society and nature.

One of the leading environmental organizations of the South, Acción Ecológica, defines ecological debt as:

> '...the debt accumulated by the Northern industrial countries towards Third World countries on account of resource plundering, environmental damage, and the free occupation of environmental space to deposit wastes such as greenhouse gases. Those who abuse the biosphere, transgress ecological limits and enforce unsustainable patterns of resource extraction of a range of natural resources must begin to discharge this ecological debt.'[9]

The debt is not necessarily a financial debt, but first and foremost an ethical and moral debt that recognizes the environmental and social consequences of centuries of colonial extraction and exploitation, and capitalist industrialization. Nonetheless, the concept of ecological debt provides a powerful tool for realigning North-South relations, and reorienting societies towards economic and ecological justice. It takes the transfer of resources from North to South out of the logic of profit, the market, or 'aid', and reframes it as a just compensation.

Slowing-down, speeding-up, and expanding

The call to transform the distorted relations between capital, society and nature comes from many different perspectives.

The Indigenous Peoples of the Andes speak of the ultimate crisis – the 'civilizational crisis' – that obliges us to re-imagine what it means to 'live well', or *vivir bien*. Bolivian President Evo Morales describes this as 'Thinking not only in terms of income per capita but also of cultural identity, community, and harmony among ourselves and with our Mother Earth.'[10]

Socialist Bellamy Foster says capitalism destroys the

'metabolism' between humans and nature. Re-establishing this metabolic relationship is, for Bellamy Foster, the key to true socialism. Mechanistic and productivist attempts at socialism ultimately failed because they ignored some essential truths: that reforming politics and institutions must begin with the real lives of people and remain in harmony with nature. I would add that reforming society means transforming social relations not only between classes but also between men and women, while also expanding individual and collective freedoms. It is, by definition, local and bottom-up.

And feminist Teresa Brennan also argues for 'the local' when she says that 'the closer to home one's energy and raw material sources are, the more one's reproduction costs stay in line: paid and domestic labor will be less exploited, the environment less depleted.'[11] Brennan also believes that 'personal productivity should be expanded and mobile, while economic productivity should be limited and self-contained.'[12] This sentiment turns the world upside down and is profoundly liberating in its implications. It means that our creative, intellectual, emotional and social selves could (and should) be enlarged while the economic is contained. This is the opposite of capitalism, where the economic defines all social relations, and in which our private selves, especially for females, are either objects of commodification or transformed into mere consumers.

Building on ideas from the workers' and feminist movements, Frigga Haug talks of a modern approach to self-liberation, which she calls four-in-one. It has shades of Karl Marx's famous vision of the communist society, where 'nobody has one exclusive sphere of activity but each can become accomplished in any branch he wishes, society... makes it possible for me to do one thing today and another tomorrow, to hunt in the morning, fish in the afternoon, rear cattle in the evening, criticize after dinner...'[13]

Four-in-one is the idea that to be fully human and free, we need to express ourselves in four dimensions: wage work, reproductive work, individual development and politics. Haug's vision is that everyone should have the possibility to engage all four aspects, but this requires a better distribution of wage work (four hours a day) and a more equal sharing of reproductive activities, like cooking or growing food or caring for families (another four hours). Third, we should have the possibility of lifelong individual development through education, music, culture, sport, or whatever (another four hours) and finally, society needs us to be politically engaged (the last four hours). After that, we can sleep. As Haug says: 'No one area should be followed without the others, since what is sought is a political constitution of life which, when carried out, would be enjoyed as truly lively, meaningful, engaging, relishing.'[14] This, she says, is a 'concrete utopia' which can serve as a compass for our political demands and strategies.

The notion that we can expand and liberate ourselves beyond our designated and sex-determined function in a system of economic production/consumption is tantalizing: it is already possible for a privileged few (and I count myself as one) but it should be possible for all, at least in my imagined world, where the commons is enlarged to encompass all, where the relationship between nature and society, between production and reproduction, and between women and men, is rebalanced, and where the wealth is shared by all, but owned by none.

Vivir bien.

Australian-born **Nicola Bullard** is a researcher, campaigner and writer with the Bangkok-based Focus on the Global South. She edits the monthly electronic *Focus on Trade* and is active in the international 'movement of movements'.

Connections: John Christensen, p 115; Richard Wilkinson & Kate Pickett, p 143; Evo Morales, p 165; Derek Wall, p 181; Danny Chivers, p 193; John Hilary, p 217.

1 Social reproduction refers to the processes involved in maintaining and reproducing people, especially labor power, on a daily and generational basis. It involves providing food, clothing, shelter and healthcare, as well as transmitting knowledge, social and cultural values, and collective and individual identity. A critique of social reproduction is central to socialist feminism. Privatization and user-pays services, stagnant wages, declining healthcare and social budgets, precarious work, and so on – all of which are endemic to neo-liberal capitalism – contribute to the crisis of social reproduction and put tremendous pressure on women, in particular. For more see Meg Luxton and Kate Bezanson (eds), *Social reproduction: feminist political economy challenges neo-liberalism*, McGill-Queen's Press, 2006. 2 John Bellamy Foster, 'Ecology and the transition from capitalism to socialism', in *Monthly Review*, November 2008. A revised version of this paper can be read at the *Links* website, http://links.org.au/node/742 3 Teresa Brennan, *Globalization and its terrors: daily life in the West*, Routledge, 2003. 4 Ulrich Duchrow and Franz J Hinkelammert, *Property for people, not profit*, Zed Books, London, 2004. 5 Ibid. 6 La Via Campesina, Statement to the UN General Assembly on the Global Food Crisis and the Right to Food, 6 April 2009, http://tinyurl.com/qk94rz 7 David Harvey, 'The right to the City', in *New Left Review*, No 53, Sep-Oct 2008. 8 John Cavanagh, Chuck Collins, Alison Goldberg, Sam Pizzigati, 'Reversing the Great Tax Shift: Seven Steps to Finance Our Economic Recovery Fairly', Institute for Policy Studies and Wealth for the Common Good, Washington DC, April 2009, see www.ips-dc.org/reports/#1207 9 Lyla Bavadan, 'The Ecological Debt', in *Frontline*, January 2004, cited at http://jades.socioeco. org/en/lbavadam.php 10 Quoted in the article 'Hugo Blanco on the Indigenous Struggle in Amazonia', *Socialist Voice*, 28 August 2008, www.socialistvoice.ca/?p=317 11 Kelly Oliver, 'Living a Tension', in *Living attention: on Teresa Brennan*, by Teresa Brennan, Alice Jardine, Shannon Lundeen, Kelly Oliver, SUNY Press, 2007. 12 Ibid. 13 Karl Marx and Fredrick Engels, *The German Ideology*. 14 Frigga Haug, 'For a life more just. The four in one perspective', downloaded from http://tinyurl.com/o2p5rl

How to Save the World, Life and Humanity

Open letter from Evo Morales, President of Bolivia, to the Fifth International Conference of Via Campesina[1], held in Maputo, Mozambique, on 13 November 2008.

Sisters and brothers

The innumerable activities that I now have as President of Bolivia prevent me from being with you, as is my constant desire. Whenever I am informed about your activities I am filled with nostalgia because, as a founder of Via Campesina, I would like to be with you debating the problems we have.

Nevertheless, in Maputo there will be representatives from Bolivia, my brothers and sisters who help me now in the struggle for a united Bolivia, that is egalitarian, without racism or discrimination. A country where there are no first- or second-class citizens and where all have the same rights and obligations, with the same possibilities to study and access healthcare, where basic services are not a private service but rather a human right.

For this reason I would like to place before you for your consideration, with much respect, the proposal I made before the United Nations, consisting of a 10-point plan to save the world, life and humanity, pulling together ideas on how to change the 'external' debt for the ecological debt, to put an end to agrofuels and the privatization of water, electricity, education and health, communication and transportation, and to create a culture of 'unity in diversity'.

First

Climate change is not the product of human beings in general, but rather the ongoing capitalist system, based on unlimited industrial development. We must do away with the exploitation of human beings and with the pillage of our natural resources. The North needs to pay the ecological debt, rather than the countries that are paying external debt.

Second

War brings profits to empires, transnational corporations and a group of families, but implies death, destruction and poverty for the peoples. The trillions of dollars destined for war should be invested in the Earth, wounded by abuse and over-exploitation.

Third

Relations of co-existence and not of submission among the countries of the world need to be achieved, free of imperialism or colonialism. Bilateral and multilateral relations are necessary because we favor a culture of dialog and of social conviviality.

Fourth

Water is a human right and for all living creatures on the planet. One can live without electricity but not without water. Water is life. It is not possible to tolerate policies that permit the privatization of water. We need an international convention on water to protect the sources of water as a human right and to avoid privatization.

Fifth

The development of clean energies friendly to nature will do away with the energy crisis. For 100 years we have been using up fossil energies created during millions of years. Avoid the promotion of agro-fuels. Land cannot be set aside for the functioning of luxury cars in the place of food production for human beings.

Sixth

No expert or specialist can debate with indigenous leaders about respect for Mother Earth. The indigenous movement ought to explain to other social sectors, urban and rural, that the Earth is our mother.

Seventh

Basic services, such as water, electricity, education, health, communication and transportation should be considered as human rights. They cannot be made private businesses since they are public services.

Eighth

Consume what is needed, prioritize what we produce and consume locally. Put an end to consumerism, decadence and luxury. It is not comprehensible that a few people can seek luxury at the expense of millions who are deprived of a decent life. While millions of people die each year from hunger, in other parts of the world millions of dollars are dedicated to combating obesity.

Ninth

Promote diversity of cultures and economies. The indigenous movement that has always been excluded is counting on unity in diversity. A plurinational State, where everyone is included within the State, white, brown, black and red.

Tenth

It is nothing new to live well. It is simply a matter of recovering the life ways of our forebears and putting an end to the kind of thinking that encourages individualistic egoism and the thirst for luxury. Living well is not living better at the expense of others. We need to build a communitarian socialism in harmony with the Mother Earth.

Evo Morales has been President of Bolivia since 2006. He is the country's first fully indigenous leader since the Spanish Conquest.

Connections: Noam Chomsky, p 33; Richard Wilkinson & Kate Pickett, p 143; Nicola Bullard, p 153; Derek Wall, p 181.

1 *Via Campesina* (from the Spanish, *la vía campesina*, 'the peasant way') describes itself as 'an international movement which co-ordinates peasant organizations of small and middle-scale producers, agricultural workers, rural women and indigenous communities from Asia, Africa, America, and Europe'. It was founded in 1992 by farmers' organizations from Europe and Latin America and had its original headquarters in Belgium. It then moved to Tegucigalpa, Honduras but is now based in Jakarta, Indonesia. The group has members in 69 countries: www.viacampesina.org

How to Take Part in the Economy

Michael Albert has developed the concept of 'parecon' or 'participatory economics'. It provides a rare model of how a classless alternative to capitalism – and to centrally planned economies as well – might actually work. In this interview with **Chris Spannos** he outlines his vision.

CS Where did parecon come from? What is its history?

MA I once heard about a strike, billed as the first, by Egyptian peasants against a Pharaoh who moved from requiring six days' labor on the pyramid a week, to requiring seven days, and from providing food to providing nothing. I think parecon harks back all the way to that uprising.

Parecon was born when revolutionaries of various camps began imagining and seeking a classless economy. That's what parecon is – a classless economy. It is not capitalism. But it is also not an economy ruled by roughly a fifth of the population that monopolizes empowering conditions. In parecon a few don't dominate the remaining participants.

Parecon itself, the model, came into being more recently, however, with a particular conception of defining institutions, when Robin Hahnel and I thought through our reactions to various schools of anti-capitalist activism, and set out our views in a book titled *Looking Forward*, about 16 years ago. Since then parecon has been repeatedly refined, partly in its conception, but mostly in how to communicate about it.

CS Is participatory economics an intellectual model or an actual system, like a place that we haven't yet visited?

MA Both. Parecon is a thing we uncover, the name of an economy that will some day exist, with real workers and consumers, flesh and blood, who produce and consume. In that sense, yes, parecon has properties like a place we haven't visited. We think about it, guess the properties, and finally uncover them.

Parecon is also, however, the name of a specific economic model, a free creation of the mind, that claims to capture the essence of the real future classless economy that we will enjoy. The model in our heads now may need to adapt and alter as we learn more about the system it seeks to clarify.

The model has a more immediate and practical purpose. It exists to provide hope by making real the demand for a new economy. It exists to provide a goal that can help us embody the seeds of the future in our current efforts, to envision an alternative economy and help us attain it. It needs to reveal the defining byways. It can, however, ignore more detailed tributaries, which will vary from case to case.

CS What are the central institutional features of parecon?

MA Workers' and consumers' self managed-councils, balanced job complexes, remuneration for duration, intensity and onerousness of socially valued labor, and participatory planning. These features are to parecon what private ownership, corporate divisions of labor, remuneration for property, power and output, and market allocation, are to capitalism. You can't have a classless economy without these defining features.

But capitalism comes in many shapes, often dramatically

different from one instance to the next. This diversity of capitalisms is not due solely to countries having different populations, resources, levels of technology. The same will hold for actual participatory economies. It will differ in the details of how labor is measured, how jobs are balanced, how councils meet and make decisions, how participatory planning is carried out.

It is a debilitating mistake to get caught up in seeking an inflexible, unvarying blueprint. Parecon is not inflexible or unvarying. It no more specifies the details of all future parecons than any broad description of capitalism's defining features tell us everything about the US, Sweden, Chile or South Africa. The model shows central defining features: no more, no less.

CS Can you start by explaining why you see self-managed workers' and consumers' councils as unavoidable if an economy is to be a parecon?

MA One of the pivotal aims of defining a post-capitalist economy is an appropriate approach to decision-making. If the economy is going to be classless and fulfill our highest aspirations, then it has to promote each worker and consumer participating in the decisions that affect their lives.

If no-one is to occupy a more privileged position than others, then each person must have the same broad relation to decision-making. There are various ways to achieve that. We could have every person get one vote in every decision, for example. But that's patently absurd. Many decisions have near zero impact on me. Why should I have the exact same say as people directly involved and far more affected? On the other hand, where I am highly involved I should have more say than people tangentially affected.

If workers and consumers are going to have an influence in outcomes proportionate to how they are affected by them, where are they going to exert this influence? It may be a lack of imagination, but I find it hard to conceive of any answer other than that workers and consumers will have to do so in gatherings.

Sometimes it seems obvious; we will make decisions as individuals, sometimes in small groups, sometimes in larger ones. We will have more or less say in decisions, either individually or in groups, depending on how much the outcomes affect us. This is the logic that leads to the idea of workers and consumers as individuals, in little teams, in whole workplaces or neighborhood councils, as well as in nested aggregates of councils, expressing their preferences.

Councils and other levels of participation should be self-managing. They should share information, discuss options, then tally preferences that give each worker and consumer a say proportionate to the degree they are affected. Sometimes people determine that democracy is best. Sometimes they decide consensus is best. Sometimes preferences are expressed by one person, or a few people, or all workers in a plant, or consumers in some locale.

The idea of workers' and consumers' councils, I should add, has a long and elevated history in labor struggle and workplace revolution – and at times also in community organizing as well. Workers and consumers gravitate to this option themselves, every time they rise in widespread resistance.

CS What about remuneration?

MA We want two things. On the one hand, we want to apportion society's output in an ethically sound way. Everyone should get an amount that reflects appropriate moral preferences, rather than violating them. Second, however, the remuneration scheme should give people economically sensible incentives. It needs to propel society's assets, without waste.

Parecon gives you more if you work longer, harder or in more debilitating conditions. You don't get more for having more power, or for owning property, or because you happen to be in an industry making something more valuable, or you have highly productive workmates, or better tools to work with.

What this approach leads to is equity. We all earn at the same rate. We all earn with the same prospects. We don't exploit one another. No-one earns excessively more because no-one can work too much longer or harder than others. When someone does earn more, for those reasons, everyone agrees it is warranted. Rather than remunerating property, power, or even output, parecon opts to remunerate how hard and how long we work, and the discomfort we endure.

Work that gets income must be socially valuable. If I say: 'Pay me for the hours I spent composing music, or digging people's lawns, or playing shortstop for a ball team,' I won't be convincing. Such work, at least done by me, is not socially valued because I am unable to do it usefully. I just don't have those capacities. If I say, instead: 'Pay me for the hours I spend producing bicycles, or producing medicine, or maybe even writing social commentary,' and it is a product that society wants and that I am capable of usefully producing, then I can get paid for my effort. But I can't just stand around and say: 'Hey, I worked, pay me!' I have to generate output commensurate to the time I claim to have spent.

CS You say 'balanced job complexes' are also central to classlessness.

MA We can't have our economic institutions giving some producers more power, which they use to accumulate excessive wealth, better conditions and so on. We know that if we let people own means of production and determine its use they will dominate outcomes and accumulate extreme wealth.

173

Parecon, seeking classlessness, excludes that. That much is straightforward.

But if some people do only rote, tedious, obedient labor, while other people do only work that involves empowering conditions, we will be dominated by the latter group, whom I call the 'co-ordinator class'.

If we reject having some people monopolize empowering conditions and roles, than we require a division of labor that doesn't give some people empowering and most people disempowering work. Balanced job complexes are simply a positive way to avoid a class-divided distribution of tasks.

We honor expertise, of course. But each worker does a mix of tasks, not solely rote or solely empowering, so that everyone is prepared to participate in self-managing councils.

CS Why must an economy have participatory planning? Wouldn't it be easier to stick with markets or to opt for central planning?

MA Well, it would certainly be an easy approach, but I think a wrong one. Both markets and central planning have flaws which compel workers and consumers to make choices contrary to classlessness. Central planning gives excessive influence to planners and diminishes the influence of others. Additionally, the former bend decisions to advance their interests, not those of workers. With markets the story is similar, but in some respects even worse. Markets induce class rule. In the rush to capture market share, to avoid being out-competed, it is necessary to cut costs. This requires a group that is callous to general needs and doesn't suffer the losses that penny-pinching imposes.

More fully explored, this provides reasons to be a market abolitionist – and to join the generalized chorus against central planning, too.

But why adopt participatory planning? The underlying

argument is not complex. We want social behavior, not anti-social behavior. We want self-management, which means informed participation. We want all the true social costs and benefits to be accounted for. These desires lead toward having those affected by decisions – the workers and consumers in their councils – co-operatively negotiate outcomes. Workers and consumers express preferences. They have to take into account what others express. There is thus a back-and-forth dynamic to it.

Participatory planning is the anarchist and decentralized socialist injunction that workers and consumers should decide production and consumption themselves, in accord with their needs and desires, not compelled by those of some narrow élite or ruling class.

CS Shouldn't many more people be discussing, debating and advocating parecon?

MA When first presented, parecon was utterly invisible – as is true with any conceptual model or argument at its outset. But things are now changing for the better. Steadily, more people come into contact with parecon and begin to assess it for themselves.

Why has this process taken so long? Why, even now, is there little print discussion and debate, even as growing numbers of activists at the grassroots are taking parecon seriously?

Well, there is relatively little written about *any* economic vision, period. I suspect vision-aversion is a big part of the problem. Make some new claim about how capitalism works, or racism, or whatever, and it will be dissected *ad nauseam*. Make some claim about what should replace capitalism, racism or whatever, and there will be a crescendo of silence.

Then again, if parecon becomes widely advocated on the Left there will arise pressure for changes in Left institutions. There is a loose but instructive analogy to the rise of feminism or black power. As those broad perspectives gained strength there arose great pressures to reduce racism and sexism in Left movements. There also arose considerable resistance, not least from people who saw them as threatening.

I think the same holds for parecon. Those who own or administer Left projects, publications and movements often realize that, if pareconish economic views become preponderant, their current agendas would be disrupted by a drive toward equity, self management and, particularly, balanced job complexes.

Whatever the causes may be, the relative absence of people seriously debating parecon's merits greatly hinders its spread. A potential reader thinks to him or herself: 'Should I wade through this book? Should I immerse myself in this website? Should I work to understand these ideas? Well, perhaps I shouldn't. After all, my favorite journals haven't said anything about it. I will wait and see if parecon gains credibility before I invest my time in assessing it.'

The rise in the numbers of people relating to parecon despite the absence of discussion and debate is arguably remarkably quick, rather than slow.

CS What difference can parecon make now?

MA If it were just for the future, why work on it now? We need vision, economic and otherwise, to overcome the cynicism that says there is no alternative to oppressive conditions. We need vision, economic and otherwise, to give us insight, permitting us to incorporate the seeds of the future in our present. And we need vision, economic and otherwise, so that our efforts lead where we want to wind up – rather than taking us in circles or, worse, toward a new world we didn't anticipate or desire.

I am baffled when people say vision has no implications. To me it is like saying to someone looking for their terminal at the airport: 'Hey, where you want to go has no relevance. Just tell me how you are feeling about where you are. That is enough to decide your terminal.' How many times must people suffer the disasters of directionless activism before we elevate having a destination to priority importance?

CS Why would it have mattered, for example, if lots of Argentineans had been advocating parecon during their uprisings?

MA In Argentina people occupied workplaces and neighborhoods, setting up what they called assemblies. In the assemblies they then began to reorient behavior and policy. They did not have a clear goal for society or the economy. They were rebelling against horrendous conditions and prospects, but not for a shared alternative. In time, most of the energy dissipated. Only very modest gains persisted. Instead of having an endless cacophony of seemingly divergent desires in play, the presence of vision would have yielded coherence, solidarity and purpose. It would take more than my knowledge of Argentina, and more time than we have, to list the large and small ways that people would have acted differently had there been an overarching shared vision.

CS What about in Venezuela?

MA Again, I hesitate to comment on a situation about which I know very little. But, in broad terms, I think the Bolivarian approach is very innovative. It seeks to avoid head-on conflict and to use the power of the Government as well as gigantic oil revenues to create parallel structures to those from the past. It believes that by displaying social concern and solidarity the new ways will replace the old, in time. In general, if you look at the Bolivarian policies to date, they are by and large incredibly inspiring and innovative. At the same time, there is a high degree of confusion about where it is all going. I think the change that would come with a coherent shared vision would be much more clarity about choices and how they are advocated, not just in the government but – much more important – in the broad population. It would, as a result, be both more involved in the process and more vigilant against its corruption.

CS What are the strategic implications of embracing positive political, cultural and kinship perspectives?

MA If we are seeking new relations for race, religion, culture, kinship, family and socialization, as I certainly think we ought to, a much-needed step is to arrive at a convincing shared vision for each realm, not just for the economy. Parecon points toward values that might transfer well to these other realms. Equally, parecon's economic features must help to attain desired aims in those other realms.

CS What are the next steps?

MA The thing about history is that it isn't even a little like chemistry or physics. There are countless possibilities, endless circles of variables piled on variables. Even tiny and quite unpredictable shifts can magnify. I have to say, honestly: who knows? Shit happens. So do good things. I guess the bottom line is that we will see what occurs – or, more accurately, we will try things and experience the results.

Michael Albert is co-editor of ZNet, and co-editor and co-founder of Z *Magazine*. He is the author of *Parecon: life after capitalism*, Verso, London, 2004.

Chris Spannos is on the staff of Znet.

This is an edited extract of an interview on Michael Albert's Zspace Page www.zmag.org/zspace/ Reprinted with permission.

Connections: David Ransom, p 11; Richard Wilkinson & Kate Pickett, p 143; Derek Wall, p 181.

PETER STALKER

TAREK EL DIWANY

VANESSA BAIRD

WALDEN BELLO

SUSAN GEORGE

NAOMI KLEIN

CHO

Open Source
Anti-Capitalism

Capitalism, despite its excesses and present problems, usually appears to be an effective means of putting bread on the table. It can be difficult to imagine another system of producing and distributing goods and services, especially after the fall of the Berlin Wall in 1989 and the collapse of the Soviet Union. Capitalism motivates and organizes production. It seems easier to picture how capitalism might be reformed so it works better rather than putting together an alternative system of production, distribution and consumption. Capitalism, it is often suggested, has been distorted and a measure of government intervention can set it right. The current recession, the worst crisis capitalism has seen since the 1930s, has increased calls for a better regulated system in which esoteric financial instruments, Ponzi pyramid investments and dodgy property deals, might all be dealt with through more effective oversight from the state.

Capitalism, though, suffers from some fundamental defects. Perhaps most fundamentally, it has a built-in growth imperative and it is difficult to see how ever-increasing economic growth is ecologically possible. Capitalism, as the present economic crisis shows, can only function if we consume more and more. Yet increasing consumption is at the root of a multiplying number of severe environmental problems from crashing fish stocks to wrecked ecosystems and of course climate change. Capitalism only really functions when consumption is growing. The present downturn in the global economy illustrates this point. Consumers are buying less, so producers are threatened with closure. In turn, unemployment is growing. The solution proposed is to increase consumer spending yet such consumption has an ecological cost, which is becoming more and more difficult to pay.

Capitalism is also based on enclosure. It fences off resources and makes us pay for them. If capitalists could make us pay for fresh air, they would. Capitalism, rather than functioning simply as a market-based system that guarantees the production of goods and services, tends to dominate every aspect of life. Capitalism may be based on human action, but it has increasingly inhuman consequences, dominating and controlling what we do. Government policies are based on what is functional for the capitalist economy, not what is necessarily good for human beings and the rest of nature. Finally, it has long been observed that capitalism functions on the sweat of the majority of humanity who work for a minority who own the means of production.

Economic systems are based on property rights. With a different system of property rights, a different and sustainable economy is possible. In capitalism, private property is the norm and property tends to become concentrated in the hands of fewer and fewer individuals. Those who lack property have to work increasingly hard to survive. The alternative to private property is usually seen as state control of resources, which in the Soviet Union and Eastern Europe proved to be bureaucratic, inefficient and ecologically damaging.

However, there is an alternative to both capitalist and state control, known variously as social sharing, open source or commons. It is based on free access to resources. If you have walked on a beach or used the internet, you have participated in the commons. The economist Elinor Ostrom has examined how commons have been used to maintain forests, rivers, seas and pastures across the globe. In 1992, *The Ecologist* magazine published 'Whose Common Future?' which argued that commons rather than state control or privatization was the best way of preserving ecology. The creation of the world wide web, the internet and free software during recent years has accelerated the importance of commons-based systems. The legal theorist Yochai Benkler has developed a commons-based system of economics known as social sharing.

The commons is ancient. It is found in Jewish and Muslim traditions. It is used universally by indigenous peoples across five continents. It was recognized in Roman law and, although often forgotten by the Left, commons, rather than state socialism, is the basis of much of Marx's critique of capitalism and inspired his thirst for communism. One of Marx's first pieces of political journalism, 'Debates on the Law on Thefts of Wood', examines the destruction of a commons system by powerful landowners.

In agricultural societies, 'customary law dictated that the community as a whole controlled the resource base. Individual proprietary rights were automatically granted to those who worked the land, provided they fulfilled the incumbent ritual and ecological obligations. This principle of land stewardship is enshrined in the traditional law or *adat*, a concept that has moral, legal, and religious implications'.

Examples of commons that work to conserve forests, grazing land, seas and other vital environments could be multiplied here but commons is also applicable to other kinds of resources. *The Economist* notes that communal property is advancing in a knowledge economy: 'Most people who use computers have heard of the "open source" movement, even if they are not sure what it is. It is a way of making software (and increasingly, other things as well), which relies on the individual contributions of thousands of programmers. The resulting programs are owned by no-one and are free for all to use. The software is copyrighted only to ensure it remains free to use and enhance. In essence, therefore, open source involves two things: putting spare capacity (geeks' surplus time and skill) into economic production; and sharing.'

A commons approach has a number of attractions. Because it promotes sharing, it has the potential to increase prosperity – defined crudely as access to material resources – while reducing resource use. In capitalism privatized ownership means that wasteful over-consumption is part of the system. With social sharing we can gain access to goods without necessarily owning them. Libraries are an excellent example of the commons approach to prosperity. Instead of buying every book we might want to read, cluttering space and cutting down trees, we can borrow books, read them and take them back. Libraries do not prevent us buying books but they mean more people can read more books while consuming far fewer resources than if we all had our own private collections.

Car pooling is also an example of social sharing. Car clubs mean that individuals who occasionally need a car can have access to them without everyone buying a car. Social sharing could be extended to all manner of goods and services. Social sharing does not eliminate private ownership but it does mean we could use fewer resources while enjoying more access to goods. The internet and the web provide numerous examples with which we are increasingly familiar.

Social sharing is based on *usufruct*. This rather ugly Latin-derived word means simply that an individual may have access to a resource on the condition that it is left in at least as good a state as one found it. Usufruct, which is found in Roman law and is the principle behind almost all commons, is a built-in ecological principle. We can borrow the car from the car pool but must leave it in a decent state for the next driver. We can use the resources of our planet only if we leave them intact for the next generation. Under usufruct, minerals and metals could only be mined if the miners guaranteed to leave the land where the mine was situated in at least as good a condition as it was found. Usufruct provides the legal basis of ecological sustainability. In contrast, private owners tend to exploit for short-term gain with little thought for new generations.

Commons throughout history have been managed, where necessary, to guarantee this ecological principle. Stinting is used to rotate access to commons so they are not exhausted by over-exploitation. In Europe, common land, rather than being a free-for-all, was managed by local committees who shared out grazing access so that land remained fertile, generation after generation. Post nonsense on a wiki and you risk being banned by the community of users.

Commons-based systems tend to be decentralized, which means they can cope with the huge amount of information required to run an efficient economic system. Decentralization is also an ecological virtue, since local people have both the motivation and the means to maintain resources ecologically. If they ruin their resources they will find it difficult to sustain living standards in the future. In turn, ecological systems are complex and local people are likely to have learned how to manage them better than distant planners. Global management lacks flexibility. Capitalism, while promoted by free marketers as a decentralized and flexible system, evolves into a planned and centralized corporate grid. Open source systems are democratic, providing each person with access to resources. Capitalism tends to concentrate resources into the hands of ever smaller numbers of people but assumes that wealth will somehow trickle down to the rest.

The peer-to-peer basis of free software development shows that collective creativity can be used to solve seemingly intractable problems. A software developer creates a product, but when it is placed free for use and development in cyberspace, others can contribute to its design. Many minds help eliminate the bugs. The creation of the world wide web for free illustrates this principle and has enabled new commons to evolve at acceleration speed. Free media are remaking the world.

To summarize, commons, by encouraging sharing, reduces both ecological damage and poverty. It is based on an ecological principle that access depends not on money or power but the ability to sustain resources. It is decentralized, democratic and creative. It has been tried and tested for much of human history. Traditionally it has been the most important form of land ownership. The creation of cyberspace means that it dominates the knowledge economy.

Even where goods and services are sold in the marketplace, a process which will shrink with the expansion of commons, capitalism can be transcended via alternative property relations that replace corporate oligarchy with economic democracy. Democracy used to be condemned as the rule of the mob, but now, however imperfectly realized, it is a universal political goal. In the same way as each citizen has one vote, in economic democracy we should have the same access to wealth. Limited companies are based on share ownership, but in a democratic economic system business enterprises could be owned by the workers. In Britain, the John Lewis group, best known for the supermarket Waitrose, is owned by its workers, who directly share in any profits made. It is not perfect but it works within capitalism as an institution that challenges traditional capitalist property rights.

In capitalism, profit is, of course, everything, but in a democratic economy, environmental and social goals could guide production. Who really enjoys working in arms manufacture or any of the numerous forms of anti-social production often necessary to make a living? In capitalism we are driven by economic insecurity to work for a corporate-owning minority, to produce goods which are often unnecessary, dangerous and ugly. William Morris, the socialist writer and designer, argued that you should not have anything in your home unless it is beautiful or useful; we could create an economy where we only work to produce things that are useful or beautiful.

I hope this thumbnail sketch has at least illustrated that there is an alternative to capitalism. To dream of an alternative to capitalism is necessary and possible, since at present we are living inside a rapidly decaying nightmare. Production, consumption and distribution of goods can be increasingly provided by commons/social sharing/open source mechanisms. Much economic activity can be decommodified, and where this is difficult, production can occur in a system of mutual ownership that rewards workers, who after all do the work. Such co-operative production can be based on ecological and social goals. The formal economy would shrink and of course work sharing could be encouraged.

A post-capitalist economy will not mean the end of history. Conflicts will occur, battles over resources will not be abolished, arguments will rage over what is meant by terms like 'ecology', 'socially necessary', 'democratic', 'useful and beautiful'. The powerful will no doubt try to destroy commons as they have done throughout history or to bend them to suit minority interests. Class struggle, if class is seen as based on access to resources, will continue. State intervention will be necessary to run postal services, energy transmission, welfare systems and much else besides. Markets no doubt, albeit in a different form, will continue. Contradictions cannot be smoothed out by rhetoric. However, as an alternative to commons, a capitalist economy does not make sense. Any economic system that demands infinite growth is eventually faced by collapse. Commons, rather than being stagnant, by respecting ecological cycles, have the potential to exist generation after generation. Capitalism does not have this ability – the numbers don't add up for our current economic arrangements.

If the economic system works, then everything else tends to follow. If it works to destroy the environment, accelerate injustice and imprison human creative power, no amount of tinkering will lead to a sustainable and just system. Global agreements on climate, for example, are necessary but they are hardly likely to work if the planet has an economic system that is based on infinite resource use.

Policies can and should be adapted to help fertilize the growth of commons-based alternatives. My 10-point policy plan would include:

1 Defending indigenous control of rainforests and other vital ecosystems;
2 Allowing workers to take control of bankrupt businesses;
3 Using government bail-outs to mutualize resources;
4 Making arms and SUV conversion an essential element of a Green New Deal;
5 Legislating for open source patenting;
6 Land reform;
7 Massive funding for libraries and other forms of social sharing;
8 Making the tax and welfare system support commons;
9 Reforming competition to transform ownership;
10 Social ownership of pharmaceuticals and medicine.

These 10 points could easily become 20 or 100 but these demands would help move us towards an alternative system. The first is by far the most urgent. The severe threat of climate change is accelerated by the destruction of rainforests and other key ecosystems, being bulldozed for mining, oil exploration and now for biofuels. If rainforest access and use were permitted under indigenous control, this would have a massive and immediate effect on reducing and eventually reversing climate change. At present, indigenous people have no role in official policy-making on climate change. This must change, since any attempt to deal with climate change that ignores the indigenous is inadequate.

As Naomi Klein and Avi Lewis have chronicled in 'The Take', an Argentinean law to allow workers to take control of bankrupt companies has increased workers' control of companies and inspired similar schemes in other Latin American countries. Similar legislation in other countries would be a vital part of building a mutual economy. The vast sums used to bail out banks and other companies could be utilized to transform patterns of ownership. In fact the financial institutions which have best survived the current economic crisis have tended to be mutuals or co-operatives such as Britain's Cooperative Bank. There is already an open source bank, Zopa, based on peer-to-peer principles, with individuals agreeing their own interest rates for borrowing and lending. Car companies are pleading for government bail-outs and we are being urged to buy new cars. Back in the 1980s, in similar circumstances, Mike Cooley, a trade union shop steward at Lucas Aerospace, put together a shopfloor plan for alternative production. A Green New Deal should be based on conversion of destructive and outdated products under workers' control.

Land reform is necessary to create new commons. Access to land under usufruct principles is vital to combating poverty while maintaining ecology. Imperial thieves have been stealing the British commons ever since William of Normandy invaded in 1066, and it is time to give the land back to the people. There have been many other Williams across the globe. As the author of *The Godfather* reminded us, behind every great fortune is a great crime.

Support for all manner of libraries and social sharing projects would be valuable. Transforming welfare by introducing a citizens' income would accelerate the creation of a new economy. Patents and copyright legislation could be reformed to extend the already phenomenal growth of a free knowledge economy. The use of patents to create obscene monopoly profits at the expense of the sick is unacceptable. Patent reform could create cheap healthcare on a planetary scale.

I am far from convinced that the powers-that-be will roll over and create a post-capitalist economy based on a number of back-of-the-envelope transitional demands. It is important to engage with the actual struggles on the ground. Everywhere you look, once sensitized to the concept, battles over commons and against enclosure can be found.

One battle occurred in 2008 when Peru's government, as part of a free trade agreement with the US, proposed a law to make it easier for corporations to buy communal indigenous land. The law would have accelerated the destruction of the Amazon, increasing climate change via logging, mining and oil exploration. Over 50 different indigenous groups decided that they would not wear this. They took nonviolent direct action, including cutting energy supplies to the cities, and, despite being threatened with military intervention, they stood their ground and forced the Peruvian Congress to repeal the law. The indigenous defend the commons and by doing so help defend global ecology.

An alternative to capitalism is both possible and necessary. It is already growing, but for it to grow enough will demand political struggle. Workers in Argentina, indigenous people in Peru and computer geeks everywhere are part of that struggle. The idea of the commons provides a living alternative that can provide prosperity without ecological destruction. So inscribe on your banners: 'Defend, extend, deepen the Commons'. We can move from a supposedly 'free market economy' to an economy which is simply free.

Derek Wall is a founder of the Ecosocialist International and Green Left and is a former principal speaker of the British Green Party. He has written a number of books on green politics. He works closely with Hugo Blanco, the Peruvian green activist who publishes *Lucha Indigena* (Indigenous Struggle).

Connections: David Ransom, p 11; George Monbiot, p 109; Richard Wilkinson & Kate Pickett, p 143; Nicola Bullard, p 153; Evo Morales, p 165; Michael Albert, p 169.

GEORGE
MONBIOT

PETER
STALKER

TAREK EL
DIWANY

VANESSA
BAIRD

WALDEN
BELLO

SUSAN
GEORGE

Climate Choices

Danny Chivers casts an eye over the options for climate justice.

Imagine 10 rabbits lost at sea, in a boat carved out of a giant carrot.

The carrot is their only source of food, so they all keep nibbling at it. The boat is shrinking rapidly – but none of them wants to be the first to stop, because then they'll be the first to starve. There's no point in any of them stopping unless everyone stops – if even one rabbit carries on eating, the boat will sink.

This is the international climate crisis in a (Beatrix Potter-flavored) nutshell: action by individual nations achieves little unless we all act together. Of course, reality is a little more complex. While it's easy to imagine the rabbits reaching a simple agreement where they all learn to dredge for seaweed instead, our situation involves massive global inequalities, differing levels of responsibility, and a history of exploitation and broken international promises.

Perhaps, then, we shouldn't be too surprised that the international climate negotiations – which began in earnest in 1990 with the talks that created the UN Framework Convention on Climate Change (UNFCCC) – have not yet got us a workable global solution. The best we've managed so far has been the 1997 Kyoto Protocol, under which industrialized nations (known as 'Annex 1' countries) pledged to cut their CO_2 emissions by a completely inadequate 5.2 per cent by 2012. The US famously pulled out of the deal, and most of those who remained in are unlikely to achieve even these small cuts.

Meanwhile, no definite plan has been agreed for ensuring that the poorer nations switch to a climate-friendly development path. The US says it won't play unless, in the name of 'fairness', all non-Annex 1 countries also take on emissions reduction targets. Southern governments, however, point out that they've arrived late to the fossil-fuel party: the industrialized nations got us into this mess by emitting, over the past 200 years, the vast majority of the greenhouse gases currently warming up the atmosphere. How can the Annex 1 countries demand that the South restrict its development with tough carbon targets when the North has mostly missed its own Kyoto goals?

At the same time, despite promised funds to support low-carbon development, to adapt to the impacts of climate change, and to transfer to low-carbon technology, the only real money flowing from North to South through the UNFCCC process has been via the highly flawed Clean Development Mechanism (CDM). This has allowed wealthy nations to offset their domestic emissions with such 'clean development' projects as urban landfill sites, giant dams that were being built anyway, and slightly more efficient steel refineries. There are now near-universal calls for the CDM to be reformed, or scrapped altogether and replaced with something fairer.

With Kyoto limping to the end of its life, governments are feverishly trying to strike a new deal on global emissions cuts between 2012 and 2020. At the time of writing (mid-2009) they're thrashing it out in meetings in Bonn, with the aim of signing an agreement at the next big Conference Of Parties

(COP) – Copenhagen, 1-12 December 2009.

Efforts have been focused on getting the US – responsible for 30 per cent of current emissions – to sign up. But a deal that favors the interests of wealthy nations over the real needs of the world's people would fail on two crucial counts. The expanded carbon market demanded by the US and the EU would enrich private traders at the expense of lives and livelihoods in the South; meanwhile, any deal without a strong justice element would almost certainly be rejected by many Southern governments.

Poorer nations have fought bitterly to enshrine a 'right to development' and an acknowledgement of countries' 'common but differentiated responsibilities' within Kyoto, which means that richer countries are expected to act first. Unless the Annex 1 countries start showing real commitment to these principles – through deep domestic emissions cuts, strings-free funding, technology transfer and development allowances – the chances of the South staying on board with a post-2012 deal are slim.[1]

Unfortunately, the trend has so far been in the opposite direction. As the climate talks have progressed from Toronto (1988) to Kyoto (1997) to Bali (2007), the rich countries' targets have been weakened by around 1,900 million tonnes of CO_2, and the role of carbon trading has grown steadily.[2]

For example, a major subject at the 2008 Poznan talks was the REDD initiative (Reduced Emissions from Deforestation and Degradation), which proposes that the carbon stored in the world's forests be added to the carbon market.[3] In one fell swoop, forest lands where people have lived for thousands of years would be commodified and sold from beneath them, generating credits to allow wealthy Northerners to carry on driving and shopping – despite the fact that new research has revealed that recognizing indigenous forest people's land rights would cost less and be more effective than using the carbon markets.[4]

WHAT'S ON THE TABLE?

Here are some of the main proposals and how they measure up [marks out of ten] when it comes to climate justice.

'Grandfathering' of Kyoto Targets
What is it?

A delightfully twee name for the way industrialized countries' emissions targets have been allocated through the UNFCCC – everyone has to reduce their emissions a certain percentage below the amount they were emitting in 1990.

Fairness (2/10) Countries that were big polluters in 1990 get to stay as big polluters, with a slight percentage cut. A fairer system would instead be based upon per capita emissions (such as the 'Contraction and Convergence' model championed by the Global Commons Institute), historical responsibility for emissions, and/or ability to pay.

Effectiveness (2/10) The 1990 baseline is completely arbitrary, with no relation to climate science.

Current support (10/10) The EU is proposing a new target of a 30 per cent emissions cut by 2020 for Annex 1 countries. The coalition of Least Developed Countries (LDCs) has said it would prefer that to be a 45-50 per cent cut. Both of these targets are against the 1990 baseline – it's just being taken for granted. Alternative ideas such as 'Contraction and Convergence' are sometimes discussed, but not acted upon.

It's a bit like...

A group of wealthy tourists and destitute refugees have survived a plane crash and are stranded on a mountain. They decide to ration out the food based on how much each person ate in the week before the crash – the more you ate per day back then, the more food you get now.

www.gci.org.uk

Greenhouse Development Rights (GDRs)
What is it?
An alternative method for setting carbon targets. It assumes that everyone on the planet below a certain income threshold should first have the right to get themselves out of poverty and are therefore exempt from any emissions targets. Responsibility for climate action is then allocated to countries based on how many of their citizens are above the income threshold, how far above it they are, and how much greenhouse gas that country produces.

Fairness (8/10) Includes an explicit 'right to develop' for the world's poor (North and South), while ensuring that wealthy Southern élites are not excluded from responsibility. However, it doesn't acknowledge historical responsibility or the 'offshoring' of emissions by wealthier countries, and there are many potential devils lurking in the details – such as how to set the income threshold.

Effectiveness (9/10) The targets within the framework are based on up-to-date climate science, and if they were met it would give us a decent shot at avoiding the worst stuff.

Current support (4/10) Some G77 governments have talked about it, and it's gained the backing of Christian Aid and Oxfam, but as yet has no official position within the UNFCCC process.

It's a bit like...
A city is razed to the ground by alien invaders. The people who escaped unscathed because they lived in solid houses built from money they stole from the aliens (thus provoking the attack) are expected to take on most of the rebuilding work. The people who had left the aliens alone, stayed poor, and lived in rickety houses that collapsed on them during the attack are allowed to recover in hospital before joining in the work.

www.ecoequity.org

Other Methods For Divvying Up Emissions and Setting Targets:

Historical Responsibility: The idea that the total emissions emitted by a country since the industrial revolution should be used as a measure of how much that nation is to blame for global climate change. Gives a good sense of how much climate change has actually been caused by that country throughout history. Frequently cited by Global South governments but very difficult to use as a basis for future targets without using lots of estimates and complex calculations – Brazil had a go once, but it never really caught on.

Carbon Intensity: The amount of carbon dioxide produced per dollar of GDP. An interesting measure but useless for setting meaningful targets because it doesn't relate directly to total emissions. Nonetheless, when the US pulled out of Kyoto in 2002, they said they were going to cut America's carbon intensity by 18 per cent in 10 years instead. They seem to be roughly on track to do this, but as their GDP has risen at the same time their overall emissions have continued to grow steadily. So that was a big help, then.

Emissions Trading

What is it?

It's the main way in which wealthy industrialized countries are planning to meet their reduction targets – by trading 'carbon credits' (permits to pollute) with other countries. Forests are due to be added to the scheme at Copenhagen.

Fairness (1/10) The system allows polluting industries and governments to buy their way out of their carbon commitments, using complex trading rules written by Northern economists. Private trading firms get rich by buying and selling the rights to the carbon in other people's forests and fields, investing in dodgy quick-fixes and propping up polluting industries.

Effectiveness (2/10) The EU Emissions Trading Scheme has yet to produce any proven emissions reductions. Wealthy governments and companies can avoid difficult-but-vital domestic emissions cuts by buying (both real and imaginary) carbon reductions from elsewhere. Politicians get an excuse not to stump up desperately needed cash for more effective low-carbon development in the Global South.

Mad, bad, and dangerous effects (8/10) Want to unleash a genetically modified carbon-munching microbe, create a famine-inducing agro-fuel plantation, privatize a forest or build a few nuclear power stations? The carbon market is the place for you!

Current support (9.5/10) It's currently Obama's favorite 'solution', and a joint US-EU trading scheme is in the works. Unless, of course, we take action to stop it.

It's a bit like...

Handing control of the Earth's vital natural systems over to a bunch of grinning Wall Street traders. Oh no, wait: it's exactly like that.

www.carbontradewatch.org
www.thecornerhouse.org.uk

Reduced Emissions from Deforestation and Degradation (REDD)

What is it?

A major discussion topic at Poznan. The latest proposal involves adding the carbon stored in forests into the carbon market, allowing countries to generate emissions permits by NOT chopping down their forests.

Fairness (2/10) In one fell swoop, forest lands where people have lived for thousands of years would be commodified and sold from beneath them, generating credits to allow wealthy Northerners to carry on driving and shopping.

Effectiveness (4/10) Protecting the forests is vital for preventing climate disaster – deforestation is currently responsible for about 20 per cent of global carbon emissions. However, inclusion in a trading scheme would mean these savings would be canceled out by extra emissions elsewhere in the world. Meanwhile, new World Bank-funded research has revealed that recognizing indigenous forest people's land rights would cost less and be more effective than using the carbon markets.

Mad, bad, and dangerous effects (6/10) Quantifying the carbon in forests is incredibly difficult. Whatever carbon value is placed on a patch of jungle will be scientifically dubious, but then used to justify an equal amount of emissions elsewhere.

Current support (5/10) This is very contentious and hotly debated within the UNFCCC process. Southern countries may eventually be forced to agree to it if other sources of forest protection funding don't show up.

It's a bit like...
'Your house is now an important carbon sink and has been used to justify 200 Australians driving to the mall. Don't worry, follow these rules and we'll still let you live here... for now.'

http://thereddsite.wordpress.com/
http://tinyurl.com/62cbca
www.redd-monitor.org

Mitigation and Adaptation Funds
What is it?
The G77 (a coalition of, confusingly, about 130 developing countries) and China are proposing that the wealthiest countries put the climate change support money they've been promising

(for years) into a central fund for spending on low-carbon technology, emission reductions and climate change adaptation in the Global South.[5]

Fairness (7/10) Putting it into a central fund has pros and cons: paying it straight to governments instead could lead to corruption and squandering on unhelpful projects, but the central fund takes the decision even further away from those affected by it.

Effectiveness (5/10) Will the funds be spent on effective projects such as protecting the land rights of indigenous forest people, or on expensive distractions like nuclear power?

Current support (7/10) The wealthy nations are going to have to hand something over if they don't want the talks to collapse completely.

It's a bit like...
The guy who drove a bulldozer through your house and sold off the rubble has promised to buy you a tent in compensation. As a huge storm gathers on the horizon, you post him another stiff reminder letter.

Technology Transfer
What Is It?
Another hot topic at Poznan. The industrialized nations pledged to give access to low-carbon technology to the developing countries. They haven't really done much about it yet – with international patenting rules being a major stumbling block.

Fairness (8/10) It's clearly fair and clearly necessary – especially the relaxing of patenting rules.

Effectiveness (6/10) It has to happen in some form if we're going to avoid disaster – but providing the means to make solar heating systems would have a different impact from, say, helping to build new nuclear power stations. The type of technology transferred will be crucial.

Current support (7/10) Southern countries are pushing hard for this, but questions remain around when, how much, and what strings will be attached.

It's a bit like...

The bloke who knocked your house down gives you a bicycle so you can pedal desperately away from the approaching storm.

Kyoto2

What is it?

A new proposal, where companies wishing to drill for oil or gas or dig up coal would have to purchase permits. These permits would be tightly restricted, and fall each year in line with the demands of climate science. The money from the permit sale would go into a global fund to protect forests, pay for adaptation measures, create a 'revolution' in sustainable technology and help poorer communities make the transition to a low-carbon world.

Fairness (7/10) The polluters pay, and the money goes to the people and places that need it. All pretty good – so long as the poor are protected from sudden fuel price rises, and the institutions charged with distributing the funds (Oliver Tickell, who developed the proposal, suggests UN agencies and NGOs) do so in a transparent and accountable way that actively includes the affected communities.

Effectiveness (8/10) It looks good on paper, and is based on solid climate science. However, we all know how adept fossil fuel companies are at finding loopholes...

Current support (1/10) This new proposal would involve totally changing the terms of the international negotiations, shifting the responsibility from countries to corporations (including a lot of state-owned companies). Will it be seen as a distraction from the main debate, a Northern-biased proposal that doesn't explicitly recognize historical responsibility, or a neat way out of the current deadlock?

It's a bit like...
That moment near the end of a meeting where someone suggests an interesting new idea that might make the previous four hours of discussion completely irrelevant, and you don't know whether to shake their hand or throw the water jug at them.

www.kyoto2.org

Government-Funded Climate Programs
What is it?
Publicly funded schemes to tackle climate change – from revamped public transport networks to mass home insulation to giant offshore wind farms.

Fairness (5/10) Depends on how much you trust your government. Publicly owned climate solutions are more accountable to the people they affect than corporate or consumer-driven solutions (in democratic states, at least). However, there's also plenty of scope for corruption and the siphoning of public funds into expensive 'solutions' that benefit wealthy élites rather than the climate.

Effectiveness (5/10) Utterly dependent on the details. However, there are some things, such as legislating against corporate polluters, and reforming national transport and energy networks, that people and community groups cannot do alone, and governments will need to play an active role.

Current support (6/10) There are positive examples out there (such as Germany's big renewables roll-out), but they are often canceled out by the simultaneous development of roads, runways and fossil-fuel power stations.

It's a bit like...
Asking a big kid you don't really like or trust to chase away some bullies for you.

Carbon Taxes
What is it?
A government tax on sources of carbon pollution.

Fairness (5/10) Could hit the poorest in society hardest through higher fuel prices, unless it were carefully designed. Taxes on companies producing or burning fossil fuels could be fairer, if those companies were prevented from passing those costs on to others. British Columbia's new carbon tax includes a rebate for the poorest families.

Effectiveness (6/10) Sweden, Finland, the Netherlands, Denmark, Germany, Norway, Italy, and a few US towns and counties have experimented with carbon taxes, with mixed results. The taxes do seem to reduce carbon emissions, but usually on a smaller scale than was hoped for – often due to loopholes and concessions demanded by industry or angry consumer groups.[6]

Current support (5/10) Carbon taxes are talked about within the UNFCCC process as a potential tool, but they're not generally very popular back home.

It's a bit like...
Asking a big kid you don't really like or trust to charge the bullies $1 for every time they thump you.

Techno-fixes and Geo-engineering
What is it?
Examples include genetically modified algal fuel, capturing CO_2 for underground storage, launching mirrors into space, discovering reliable nuclear fusion, turning food crops into agro-fuels, dumping iron in the oceans and spraying sulphates in the sky.[7]

Fairness (1/10) Most of these schemes would place disproportionate control of the global climate in the hands of a small number of companies or governments. Imagine if the US or China had control of a giant space mirror that was the only thing preventing the world from being fried, or if Monsanto held the patent for an algal fuel that the whole world relied upon for power. What a beautiful future we'd be building.

Effectiveness (2/10) Most are more than a decade away from large-scale implementation, and would drain resources away from proven and sustainable solutions.

Mad, bad, and dangerous effects (10/10) Poisonous algal blooms, disruption of little-understood oceanic food webs, mass appropriation of lands, seas and forests, acid rain, sudden future CO_2 eruptions, and corporate control of the climate system... will that do?

Current support (7/10) European governments are desperate for carbon capture to materialize. There have been pro-sulphate-spraying demonstrations in Australia. An open market in carbon emissions would be a big boost to a lot of these wacky schemes.

It's a bit like...
Your house is on fire, so you sit down in the living room and start drawing up designs for a giant wall-smashing robot.

Carbon Rationing

The idea of issuing personal carbon emission quotas to businesses and/or the public, with a national limit that gets smaller each year. An idea embraced by some (voluntary Carbon Rationing Action Groups have sprung up around the UK), and rejected by others as an infringement of civil liberties and personal freedoms. The fact that most of the schemes proposed include some form of quota-trading means that the wealthiest would be able to prolong their high-emission lifestyles by purchasing permits from the poor – although some commentators note that this could be an effective form of wealth redistribution. Others call it a privatization of the atmosphere on a par with international carbon markets. No such scheme exists anywhere yet, although some governments have talked about it.

Community Solutions

What is it?

Another ridiculously broad category encompassing community-owned sustainable energy, food and transport, and the recognition of indigenous peoples' rights to land, forests and traditional farming practices.

Fairness (9/10) Solutions designed and implemented by the people most directly affected by them are far more likely to be fair and accountable. However, if they don't also lead to major emissions reductions then millions of people round the world will still suffer from disastrous climate change.

Effectiveness (7/10) Local solutions may lead to dramatic local carbon savings but unless they are part of a wider carbon-cutting plan there's no way of guaranteeing that they'll be enough.

Current support (3/10) Most international discussions and national programs are focused on large-scale, market-driven solutions rather than supporting community initiatives. However, international social movements are starting to get active and vocal on this issue – the powerful small farmers' network La Via Campesina are issuing ever-stronger demands for 'Food Sovereignty' because 'peasant agriculture cools the planet'.[8]

It's a bit like...
Just ruddy well getting on with it.

THE ROAD AHEAD

If the talks continue in their current vein, then Copenhagen is likely to produce a similar deal to Kyoto – arbitrary (though larger) targets against a 1990 baseline, perhaps giving targets to some of the larger developing countries in return for extra mitigation funds, and with carbon trading as the main 'delivery mechanism'. It would probably end up about as successful as Kyoto, too.

Fortunately, global dissent is growing. Large NGOs such as Friends of the Earth International, Oxfam and Christian Aid are becoming increasingly vocal on the issue of climate justice. New networks are forming amongst Northern and Southern social movements to demand community-led solutions to the climate crisis, and an end to the privatization of lands and forests through carbon trading schemes.

We shouldn't get too hung up on Copenhagen – we're far more likely to create lasting change by building powerful national and international movements than by pouring all our energy into specific summit meetings. But it's hard to deny that we need some sort of international framework for tackling this global issue. Despite its flaws, the UNFCCC is the only one we've got, and the urgency of the climate issue requires us to work with it.

However, the Kyoto Protocol has been a dismal failure. Should we demand that governments scrap it completely and start again from scratch? It's tempting, but would be unlikely to gain the crucial support of Southern negotiators, who fear that a brand new deal would see them lose their hard-won 'differentiated responsibility'.

A better approach might be to create space within the existing talks for alternative, fairer systems and ideas – such as GDRs, Kyoto2, community-led solutions, indigenous rights, strings-free clean development assistance, patent-free technology transfer – to get a hearing. Currently emissions trading, private financing and market-based mechanisms are seen as the only route to greenhouse gas reductions, and are crowding everything else out of the debate.

This suggests a simple, effective starting point for developing a successful – and just – global agreement: we need to get rid of carbon trading.

Just: do it
Many groups and movements could happily unite around a major campaign to discredit the carbon markets. However, this needs to start now. The massive protests planned for Copenhagen will be too late to have much effect on the talks (unless things have gone so badly that they need to be shut down!).

Let's face it – whatever gets agreed at Copenhagen, governments are unlikely to stick to it unless there is an international movement powerful enough to make it happen. A global climate treaty will never be a panacea, but we can at least make sure it's a step towards – rather than away from – climate justice.

Danny Chivers is a writer, researcher, activist and poet on all things climate-change related. You can read more of his work at http://adaisythroughconcrete.blogspot.com.

1 T Roberts & B Parks, *A Climate Of Injustice*, MIT Press 2007. 2 Diana Liverman, 'Survival into the Future in the Face of Climate Change' in E Shuckburgh (ed), *Survival: The Survival of the Human Race* (2006 Darwin Lectures), Cambridge University Press, 2006. 3 See: thereddsite.wordpress.co 4 *The Guardian*, 'Pay indigenous people to protect rainforests, conservation groups urge', 17 Oct 2008. 5 Financial Mechanism for Meeting Financial Commitments under the Convention. Proposal by the G77 and China to the Poznan meeting. 6 Nicola Liebert, 'Why Ecotaxes May Not Be The Answer', *New Internationalist* 416, Oct 2008. 7 'Techno-Fixes' report, Corporate Watch, www.corporatewatch.org 8 Open Letter From Maputo: V International Conference of La Via Campesina, 26 Oct 2008.

Connections: Ann Pettifor, p 21; Nicola Bullard, p 153; Patrick Bond, p 211.

JOHN
CHRISTENSEN

GEORGE
MONBIOT

PETER
STALKER

TAREK EL
DIWANY

VANESSA
BAIRD

WALDEN
BELLO

GE

Carbon Charade

Carbon trading is not a seaworthy lifeboat in the turbulent waters of global warming. Patrick Bond argues that there's no substitute for community-led renewable energy.

What could be a last-ditch attempt to rely on markets to reduce greenhouse gas emissions looks likely to come from carbon-trading enthusiast, US President Barack Obama.

His market-friendly approach to tackling climate change is not surprising. Wall Street financiers donated substantially more campaign cash to Obama than McCain. In January 2008 Obama announced: 'We would put a cap-and-trade system [a carbon trading mechanism] in place that is as aggressive, if not more aggressive, than anybody else's out there... So if somebody wants to build a coal-powered plant, they can; it's just that it will bankrupt them because they're going to be charged a huge sum for all that greenhouse gas that's being emitted. That will also generate billions of dollars that we can invest in solar, wind, biodiesel and other alternative energy approaches.'

The idea is that polluters would bid against each other for a share of the emissions allowed under an agreed cap, which in turn they can trade with each other so as to improve economic efficiency.

It may sound like a neat plan. But it won't work: in part, ironically, because the financial crisis that helped sweep Obama to power has also caused the price of carbon to collapse.

The crisis crashed so many financial institutions and froze credit markets so quickly that carbon values in the emissions-trading markets plummeted by a quarter during the first weeks of October 2008, from around $30 per tonne to less than $22. The price had been $37 per tonne in July – showing just how quickly an incentive scheme meant to provide stability and security to clean energy investors can do the opposite.

A low carbon price is no good for stimulating the kind of investment in alternatives needed: for example, an estimated $50-75 per tonne is required to activate private sector investments in 'carbon capture and storage', the as-yet-non-existent technology by which coal-fired power stations could, theoretically, bury liquefied carbon emitted during power generation.

This extreme volatility makes it abundantly clear that market forces cannot be expected to discipline polluters.

Carbon trading, like most climate policies currently under consideration by élites, is what the French sociologist André Gorz would have called a 'reformist reform'. It is addressing a market-caused problem – greenhouse gases released during most capitalist transactions – with a capitalist 'solution'. That solution allows the North to continue emitting, through the granting and trading of brand new property rights to pollute. The only real winners are speculators, financiers and energy-sector hucksters who have made billions already. As the air itself is privatized and commodified, poor communities across the world suffer and resources and energy are diverted away from real solutions.

But opponents of emissions trading still need to persuade centrist greens and the broader swathes of society that the carbon market is crazy, because conventional wisdom begins with the opposite premise. As Obama himself says: 'This market mechanism has worked before and will give all American consumers and businesses the incentives to use their ingenuity to develop economically effective solutions to climate change.'

Will it really?

Canadian economist John Dales first justified trading in emissions rights by applying market logic to water pollution in a 1968 essay. Then, after the 1980s Reagan/Bush administrations neutered the US Government's ability to prohibit destructive activities, the Clean Air Act of 1990 was the first to legalize trade in sulfur dioxide to tackle acid rain. This approach was far less successful than parallel European 'command-and-control' environmental policies.

Nonetheless, in 1997, the Kyoto Protocol was negotiated to include carbon trading as a core strategy to reduce global emissions. This was because the then US Vice-President Al Gore threatened that his Congress would only sign up if corporations gained the ability to continue emitting above set limits by paying to buy someone else's right to pollute. After co-opting critics in Kyoto, the Clinton-Gore Administration and Congress did not keep their word and, later, George W Bush pulled out of Kyoto. But the idea of carbon trading stuck and in Europe the Emissions Trading Scheme (ETS) was launched in January 2005.

Ever since, tales of scandals and market mishaps have emerged from dismayed financiers and business journalists. The intrinsic problem in setting an artificially generated market price for carbon was revealed in April 2006 when the ETS crashed, thanks to the over-allocation of pollution rights. The EU had miscalculated on how to set up the market and granted electricity generation firms far too many credits. Carbon lost over half its value in a single day, destroying many carbon offset projects earlier considered viable.

By 2007, the European Commissioner for Energy had admitted the ETS was 'a failure'. Peter Atherton of Citigroup conceded: 'ETS has done nothing to curb emissions...[and] is a highly regressive tax, falling mostly on poor people.' Had it achieved its aims? 'Prices up, emissions up, profits up... so, not really.' Who wins, who loses? 'All generation-based utilities – winners. Coal and nuclear-based generators – biggest winners. Hedge funds and energy traders – even bigger winners. Losers... ahem... consumers!'

Even the *Wall Street Journal* confirmed in March 2007 that emissions trading 'would make money for some very large corporations, but don't believe for a minute that this charade would do much about global warming'.

The Kyoto Protocol also promotes carbon trading in the Majority World via the Clean Development Mechanism (CDM). This aims to finance emissions reductions project by project: for example, by turning landfill methane into electricity, or by planting trees. But, according to a *Newsweek* investigation in March 2007, 'it isn't working... [and represents] a grossly inefficient way of cutting emissions in the developing world.'

Notorious projects like the Plantar timber monoculture in Brazil secured vast funds, with dreadful consequences for local communities and ecosystems. *Newsweek* called the trade 'a shell game' which has already transferred '$3 billion to some of the worst carbon polluters in the developing world'.

In October 2008, with the market crashing, Carl Mortished wrote in *The Times* of London: 'The ETS is making a mockery of Europe's stumbling attempts to lead the world in a market-based carbon strategy. It is causing irritation and frustration to the armies of advisers and investors who seek to cajole utilities into big investments in carbon reduction.'

All this mainstream criticism should spell the end for what is clearly a bad idea. But many still doggedly endorse the carbon market, including major green groups in the influential Climate Action Network (CAN), which has lobbied most visibly on the Kyoto Protocol. Why? Some would say, pragmatism: it's the only game in town, according to Sierra Club Canada director Elizabeth May. 'I would have preferred a carbon tax, but that is not the agreement we have,' she said. 'The reality is that Kyoto is the only legally binding agreement to reduce greenhouse gases. When you're drowning and someone throws you a lifeboat, you can't wait for another one to come along.'

But according to Michael Dorsey, professor of political ecology at Dartmouth College in the US, there is another reason for CAN's support: some of its leaders have personal involvement in the industry. He lists many prominent greens closely connected to carbon-trading firms. Take, for example, CAN board member Jennifer Morgan of the Worldwide Fund for Nature, who took leave for two years to direct work on Climate and Energy Security at carbon-trading firm E3G. Or Kate Hampton, formerly of Friends of the Earth, who joined Climate Change Capital as head of policy while simultaneously advising the EU on energy and the environment, working for the California Environmental Protection Agency, and acting as president of International Carbon Investors and Services.

Dorsey concludes: 'After more than a decade of failed politicking, many NGO types… are only partially jumping off the sinking ship – so as to work for industries driving the problem. Unfortunately, many continue to influence NGO policy from their current positions, while failing to admit to or even understand obvious conflicts of interest.'

Tellingly, in November 2008, Friends of the Earth International formally withdrew from CAN membership.

The financial crisis has proved categorically that carbon trading is not a seaworthy lifeboat. As temperatures (and sea-levels) rise we are discovering the numerous leaks, opening up space for a crucial debate about how to change the world's economy into something that does not threaten our descendants' future. Luckily, countering the more sluggish, corporate-sponsored elements of the environmental movement are grassroots organizations, coming together to oppose market strategies wholesale and advocate direct and equitable measures that reverse addiction to fossil fuels.

Critics from Indonesia, Thailand, India, South Africa, Brazil and Ecuador, together with Northern academics, researchers and radical environmentalists, first issued the 'Durban Declaration' in October 2004. This sounded the alarm about the ethical and economic shortcomings in carbon trading.

A tragic setback came in July 2007 with the death of Durban Declaration host Sajida Khan. She had battled against a Clean Development Mechanism proposal for methane extraction that had kept open the Bisasar Road toxic dump next to her home – which caused the cancer that ultimately killed her. But in December 2007, the movement joined forces with broader global justice activism at the Bali climate talks and formed the Climate Justice Now! network.

Climate Justice Now! is committed to exposing the false solutions promoted by governments, financial institutions and transnational corporations – such as forest carbon markets, agro-fuels and carbon offsetting. Instead, its members are campaigning to leave fossil fuels in the ground and invest in clean, efficient, community-led renewable energy. These are the only serious strategies in place: to halt climate change at the supply side. They will go much further than market gimmicks towards saving the planet.

Patrick Bond directs the Centre for Civil Society at the University of KwaZulu-Natal in Durban, South Africa, and is co-editor of *Climate Change, Carbon Trading and Civil Society*, available from UKZN Press and Rozenberg Publishers (Amsterdam).

Connections: Vanessa Baird, p 65; Nicola Bullard, p 153; Danny Chivers, p 193.

Now, a Real Chance to Tackle Global Poverty

John Hilary sets out a people's blueprint for eradicating hunger and poverty.

At the Millennium Summit in September 2000, the world's governments pledged that they would 'spare no effort to free our fellow men, women and children from the abject and dehumanizing conditions of extreme poverty'. The Summit adopted the Millennium Development Goals (MDGs) as a blueprint for halving world poverty and hunger by 2015, with measurable targets for improving health, education, employment, environmental sustainability and gender equality.

The global economic crisis has undermined any chance of attaining these targets across the world. Up to 200 million more people will be forced into extreme poverty in developing countries as a result of the worldwide recession, according to the International Labour Organization.[1] Millions will be cast adrift into the informal economy, where they will struggle to eke out a living in the streets and markets of overburdened cities. Even in the world's richest countries, unemployment is set to rise to over 10 per cent by the end of 2010, throwing an extra 25 million people out of work.[2]

As a result of this economic meltdown, all the MDGs are now under threat. As the UN has noted in its latest progress report, rising food prices, coupled with falling family incomes, have already begun to reverse the gains achieved in alleviating malnutrition among children. Progress in reducing child mortality rates is also at risk, with particular dangers for girl children: during times of economic downturn, the increase in infant mortality among girls in developing countries is five times higher than for boys. Mortality rates among mothers may also increase as countries in South Asia and sub-Saharan Africa are forced to cut back on maternal health programs.[3]

Yet even before the current crisis, progress towards the MDGs was far from secured. Statistics released by the World Bank in 2008 revealed that there were still 1.4 billion people living in extreme poverty around the world. This measure – calculated as living below $1.25 a day – represents poverty according to what it means to be poor in the very poorest countries (Mali, Chad, Rwanda, Nepal etc). The calculation marked a major revision of the Bank's previous estimate that the total number of people living in extreme poverty worldwide had fallen below the one billion mark.[4]

These aggregate figures would be worse still were it not for China's achievements in reducing poverty levels amongst its vast population over the past three decades. As the UN and World Bank both acknowledge, without China's successes the rest of the world would be way off course in its attempts to reach the MDGs by the target date of 2015. Lumping all developing countries together obscures the fact that most other regions were already destined to fail to reach the anti-poverty goals, even before the current downturn.

Importantly, too, the World Bank's findings revealed a further 1.2 billion people living below $2 a day (the median poverty line for developing countries as a whole) but above the extreme poverty line of $1.25 a day. Not only were these people already in desperate straits, but they were shown to be in danger of slipping into the most extreme poverty if confronted with any form of shock to their household finances. The current economic crisis, coming on top of the food and fuel crises of the past couple of years, is just one such shock.

The MDGs were adopted by the international community as a minimum program, aiming not to eradicate poverty completely but to halve the proportion of people living in extreme want by 2015. The current economic crisis has torpedoed any possibility of realizing even this minimum program, as hundreds of millions more people will find themselves forced into the direst poverty as a result of losing their jobs, their homes and their livelihoods.

Yet the fact that the global economic system had already condemned 2.6 billion people (half the total population of the developing world) to poverty brings with it two main consequences. First, it means we should not be seeking to restore the previous system, which was responsible for so much injustice, but aiming to build a new one based on a set of alternative principles and policy choices. Second, it means we must seek to use the current crisis as an opportunity to press for real change.

The five-point program below represents a distillation of key principles upon which to found an alternative vision of the future. It is based on discussions at a number of joint meetings and seminars held at the national, regional and international levels since the economic crisis broke, as well as drawing on the call for a new economic and social order which came out of the 2009 World Social Forum in Belém.[5] While the text below relies on the common endeavor of those who participated in those discussions, it does not make any claim to being a record of those debates.

1 A New Model

At its most basic level, the current crisis has made clear the overriding necessity of developing a new paradigm to replace the failed model of free-market capitalism. The crisis has been caused by a distinct political agenda pursued over the past 30 years by rich country governments and the international financial institutions which have done their bidding. Despite their rhetoric at the Millennium Summit and since, these powers have adopted a set of policies which are designed not to achieve the MDGs but to further a much narrower range of self-interested objectives.

These policies have been founded on the three central pillars of the Washington Consensus: trade liberalization, privatization and deregulation of markets. The governments of the rich world have pursued these policies through multilateral channels such as the World Bank, International Monetary Fund (IMF) and World Trade Organization (WTO), in which they have long enjoyed a monopoly of power and influence. At the same time, rich nations have attempted to promote the same model through bilateral channels, whether through free trade agreements negotiated outside the framework of the WTO or as a condition of development assistance and debt relief granted on a direct basis to recipient countries.[6]

Governments have at times been candid as to their motives for these policy choices. The European Union, for example, has made no secret of the fact that its trade policy has been designed to create new business opportunities for its own industries. The European Commission – which is responsible for implementing EU trade policy – has stated that it sees the WTO's General Agreement on Trade in Services (GATS) as 'first and foremost an instrument for the benefit of business' rather than a mechanism through which to meet public policy goals, and it has engaged in the services negotiations at the WTO in open pursuit of this corporate objective. The EU's new Global Europe strategy is explicitly designed to benefit European exporters in their attempts to force open the emerging markets of the developing world.[7]

The new model to replace the Washington Consensus must reverse this prioritization of corporate interests over people's needs. Any paradigm seeking to secure the well-being of people and planet must put an end to those policies which have been designed to favor transnational capital over all other considerations. This includes a fundamental revision of all trade, investment and legal provisions which have enabled capital to profit at the expense of labor, local communities and the environment. It will also involve reintroducing controls on finance capital and prohibiting speculation on commodities such as food and natural resources. It will incorporate a binding regulatory framework at both national and international levels to hold corporations accountable for the impact of their operations, wherever they may be.

More fundamentally, however, this paradigm shift must also challenge the very model of economic growth which has been seen as inviolable up to now. The overproduction and debt-fueled consumption which have resulted from capitalist expansion over the past three decades must be reversed if we are not to see repeated economic crises and ecological catastrophe in years to come.[8] In place of the fetishization of growth, trade and consumption, we need a new model of social production designed to serve a positive set of higher goals.

This new model must in turn be based on the principles of decent work, environmentally sustainable development and the reorientation of production towards social ends. The provision of a living wage to all working women and men across the world is a crucial first step in redressing their increased exploitation and their shrinking share in national income over recent decades. Similarly, reorienting production towards socially useful ends will necessarily entail its demilitarization, including the long-term conversion of weapons manufacture to peaceful and productive purposes instead.[9]

2 Reassert the Public

Alongside this radical paradigm shift, we must reassert the importance of the public in our social and economic existence. The development of free-market capitalism has included not only geographical expansion into previously closed economies, but also the creation of new markets where needs were previously supplied on a non-market basis. This increased 'marketization' has been accompanied by the 'financialization' of most aspects of our everyday lives, so that housing, transport, health, water, food, education, labor, credit, social security and culture itself have all been appropriated and redefined as commercial activities.[10]

Reasserting the public is a necessary corrective to this process. In some cases, this may point towards nationalization or renationalization – for example, the reclaiming of public services provided by the public sector, or nationalization of the banks. In other cases, it may suggest more localized community solutions or autonomous systems of provision.[11] The key requirement is to assert the primacy of public benefit over private profit, together with the principle of democratic accountability and control.

By the same token, reclaiming public space also entails challenging the commodification of essential goods and services for sale on international markets. The most far-reaching impact of the Uruguay Round of world trade talks held between 1986 and 1994 was to expand the reach of international trade rules into areas previously considered to be outside the realm of commercial considerations. Public services, food production, cultural heritage systems and domestic legislation were all brought within the compass of world trade rules for the first time, and in many cases subordinated to those rules. Reasserting the public means taking all these essential aspects of our common life out of international markets and back into public control.

3 Justice and Redistribution

The new world order must be based on principles of justice and equity, not the profound imbalances which have condemned almost half the world's population to lasting poverty. We can no longer allow a situation where the richest two per cent of the planet own half its assets while the poorest half of the world's population owns barely one per cent of global wealth. This inequality lies at the heart of the current economic crisis, and we must begin to address the imbalance by redistributing the spoils of globalization fairly.

The first step in that process is to reverse the net flow of finance currently going from South to North. While the rich countries of the Global North still hold 90 per cent of the world's wealth (for just 18 per cent of its population), the poorest countries continue to pay them $100 million every day in debt repayments. It is time to end this scandal once and for all with full debt cancellation and a massive transfer of finance from the rich to the developing world. This should include the repayment of debts owed by the rich world to the countries of the South, including the ecological debt of climate change which has been caused by industrialized countries but will hit the poor hardest.

The same principle of redistribution must govern our system of taxation. Tax is a key part of the social contract under which companies operate in our economies, yet that contract is broken on a regular basis in developing and industrialized countries alike. Britain currently loses over £100 billion ($150 billion) a year in unpaid business taxes, while developing countries are deprived of up to £250 billion ($375 billion) each year through corporate tax dodging – five times what they receive in aid. These tax revenues are vital at the best of times for funding public services and social welfare programs, but at times of economic slowdown they become critical. A just tax regime requires a new standard of full country-by-country reporting for transnational corporations, the closing down of all tax havens and the prosecution of those engaged in aiding and abetting companies to avoid paying the taxes they owe.

At the international level, too, taxation must form a central element in the redistribution of resources from North to South. A wide range of such taxes have been proposed, including on financial transactions, on air travel and on other polluting activities. The Tobin Tax was originally conceived as a constraint on foreign currency speculation, and came into new vogue at the time of the East Asian financial crisis of 1997-98. At a minimal rate of just 0.005 per cent, a levy on foreign exchange transactions in the four major world currencies (yen, euro, US dollar and sterling) would generate over $33 billion each year for use on development projects, public services and adaptation in the face of climate change.[12]

4 Human Rights, Environmental Sustainability

The past three decades have seen a dramatic increase in the powers of transnational corporations operating in the global economy. Often these new powers have been won at the expense of the countries, the communities and the ecosystems in which companies are active. Yet world leaders have responded with no more than voluntary codes of conduct for transnational corporations, which have in turn created a 'permissive environment' for further abuses to be committed with impunity, according to Professor John Ruggie, UN special representative on business and human rights.[13] Ultimately, as recent events have made clear, the refusal to assert control over transnational capital has been responsible for the collapse of the system itself.[14]

The new global order must be founded on the prioritization of human rights and ecological integrity. Workers' rights must be restored and protected, including guarantees of decent work, a living wage and the right to form or join trade unions of their choosing. Women's rights must also form a founding principle of the new order, both in terms of their economic rights as workers and also in respect of reproductive, social and political rights. The rights of migrants and other vulnerable groups must be given particular priority in view of the increased stress put upon such people at times of economic crisis.

The right to food is of particular importance in achieving the MDGs, not least in the context of rising prices, food riots and increased hunger levels over the past couple of years. The principle of food sovereignty must form an essential element in any new order, prioritizing as it does the needs of small-scale farmers over agribusiness, the importance of long-term environmental sustainability and the common use of natural resources as opposed to the privatization of land, seeds and water.[15] Once again, this reorientation leads back to the new economic paradigm outlined above, where basic needs such as food are no longer seen as commodities from which capital can profit, but as rights which governments are obliged to guarantee to their peoples.

5 Reclaim Democratic Control

None of the above solutions will be possible as long as power rests in the hands of a few leading governments and the institutions they control. The World Bank, IMF and WTO are all dominated by the most powerful nations, and proposed reforms to their voting structures will still leave poorer countries without a voice. Despite being responsible for the free-market policies which caused the crisis, all three bodies have tried to use the current turmoil to win themselves greater powers.

Yet the institutions which presided over the 'lost decades' of development are not fit for purpose and cannot be entrusted with our future. The IMF forfeited all credibility as a result of its catastrophic mishandling of the East Asian financial crisis of 1997-98, and has continued to impose damaging economic conditions such as privatization, market liberalization and fiscal austerity on those countries which have had to turn to it for assistance – including those which have been forced to do so as a result of the current economic meltdown. Prior to its resurrection at the London summit of the G20 in April 2009, the IMF was widely considered a 'dead man walking'.[16]

The WTO faces a similar crisis of legitimacy as a result of the repeat collapses of the Doha Round of global trade negotiations, while the World Bank's dogmatic commitment to neoliberal and high-carbon solutions reflects its continued refusal to learn from its past mistakes. Suggestions that such institutions can be reformed to meet the needs of the new world order fail to appreciate the deep-rooted ideologies and interests that inform and underpin them. Instead, we need to take back control of the global economy through democratic bodies which are accountable to the people they are meant to serve.

Developing countries are already finding new ways of breaking the power of the old institutions through initiatives such as the Banco del Sur, the ALBA trade agreement and the Chiang Mai Initiative.[17] Many have called for the UN to be identified as the proper forum for deciding the future of the global economy. The UN's Commission of Experts on reforms of the international monetary and financial system, headed by Nobel laureate and former World Bank chief economist Joseph Stiglitz, has called for a new Global Economic Council under UN auspices to replace the G20. As noted by the president of the UN General Assembly, the G192 – that is, the entire membership of the United Nations – is the only body with the legitimacy to develop a truly global response to the global crisis.[18]

Conclusion

The economic crisis has opened up space for a discussion of alternatives to the neoliberal model which has dominated for the past 30 years. While the governments of the G20 have thrown vast sums of money at the problem in order to patch up and preserve the existing system, they have signally failed to address the root causes which caused the crisis in the first place. If the G20 is allowed to have its way, the failed model of free-market capitalism will live to stagger on towards its next crisis.

The mass mobilizations seen in countries across the world over past months testify to a growing sense that the dominant model of free-market capitalism can be replaced by a radically new system based on a wholly different set of principles. The constituent parts of the global justice movement have been engaged in the various struggles outlined above over many years, and have won a number of important victories in resisting the neoliberal agenda while developing positive alternatives to it. Yet system failure at the global level opens up the possibility of more fundamental change over and above the single-issue campaigns and causes which have been developed in response to particular threats.

The current moment therefore represents an opportunity to draw together the different strands of the global justice movement behind a common vision of a better world. It is an opportunity to be ambitious, to challenge the central precepts of the capitalist system at its roots and to replace it with a new set of economic power relations founded on principles of justice, redistribution and collaboration. Such a transformation will carry us far beyond the MDGs towards a new global order dedicated not to the increase of corporate profits but to the satisfaction of people's needs. It is up to us to make it a reality.

John Hilary is the Executive Director of the British anti-poverty organization War on Want.

Connections: David Ransom, p 11; Noam Chomsky, p 33; Susan George, p 49; Walden Bello, p 57; Yash Tandon p 131; Nicola Bullard, p 153.

1 *Global Employment Trends*, International Labour Organization, Geneva, Jan 2009. 2 *OECD Economic Outlook Interim Report*, Organization for Economic Cooperation and Development, Paris, March 2009. 3 *The Millennium Development Goals Report 2008*,

United Nations, New York, Sep 2008; 'Poor countries threatened with higher death and drop-out rates', UNDP, New York, 31 Mar 2009. **4** S Chen and M Ravallion, *The Developing World is Poorer than We Thought, but No Less Successful in the Fight against Poverty*, Policy Research Working Paper 4703, World Bank, Washington DC, Aug 2008; both the $1.25 figure and the $2 figure below are in terms of 2005 purchasing power parity (PPP). **5** *Let's put finance in its place!* Call for the signature of NGOs, trade unions and social movements, Belém, 1 Feb 2009; available at www.choike.org/gcrisis **6** For the former, see *Fighting FTAs: The growing resistance to bilateral free trade and investment agreements*, BIOTHAI and GRAIN, Feb 2008; for the latter, *Profiting from Poverty: Privatisation consultants, DFID and public services*, War on Want, London, Sep 2004. **7** *Where Next? The GATS 2000 Negotiations*, European Commission, Brussels, Jun 1998; *Global Europe: The European Union's double attack on developing countries and the European social model*, War on Want, London, Apr 2008. **8** Graham Turner, *The Credit Crunch: Housing Bubbles, Globalisation and the Worldwide Economic Crisis*, Pluto Press, London, 2008; Larry Elliott and Dan Atkinson, *The Gods that Failed: How Blind Faith in Markets has Cost us Our Future*, Bodley Head, London, 2008. **9** See, for example, the work and publications of the Bonn International Centre for Conversion: www.bicc.de **10** Costas Lapavitsas, *Financialised Capitalism: Direct exploitation and periodic bubbles*, paper presented to conference 'A Crisis of Financialisation?', School of Oriental and African Studies, London, 30 May 2008. **11** See examples in *Reclaiming Public Water: Achievements, struggles and visions from around the world*, Transnational Institute and Corporate Europe Observatory, Amsterdam, 2005; *Building the New Common Sense: Social ownership for the 21st century*, Left Economics Advisory Panel, London, 2008; *Triple Crunch: Joined-up solutions to financial chaos, oil decline and climate change to transform the economy*, New Economics Foundation, London, 2008. **12** Rodney Schmidt, *The Currency Transaction Tax: Rate and revenue estimates*, United Nations University Press, North-South Institute and War on Want, Tokyo, Oct 2008; see also Dean Baker, *The Benefits of a Financial Transactions Tax*, Center for Economic and Policy Research, Washington DC, Dec 2008. **13** *Business and Human Rights: Mapping international standards of responsibility and accountability for corporate acts*, Report of the Special Representative of the Secretary-General on the issue of human rights and transnational corporations and other business enterprises, UN document A/HRC/4/035, 9 Feb 2007. **14** *The Global Economic Crisis: Systemic failures and multilateral remedies*, UNCTAD, Geneva, Mar 2009. **15** Michael Windfuhr and Jennie Jonsén, *Food Sovereignty: Towards democracy in localised food systems*, FIAN International and ITDG Publishing, Rugby, Mar 2005. **16** *Structural Conditionality in IMF-Supported Programs*, Independent Evaluation Office, IMF, Washington DC, 2007; Nuria Molina and Javier Pereira, *Critical Conditions: The IMF maintains its grip on low-income governments*, Eurodad, Brussels, Apr 2008; 'Back from the dead: IMF pumps out loans and conditionality', Bretton Woods Project, London, 27 Nov 2008. **17** 'Banco del Sur to start operations with US$10bn in capital', Business News Americas, Santiago, 24 Mar 2009; David Harris and Diego Azzi, ALBA – *Venezuela's answer to 'free trade': The Bolivarian alternative for the Americas*, Focus on the Global South, Bangkok, and Hemispheric Social Alliance, São Paulo, Oct 2006; C Randall Henning, *The Future of the Chiang Mai Initiative: An Asian Monetary Fund?*, Peterson Institute for International Economics, Washington DC, Feb 2009. **18** *Recommendations by the Commission of Experts of the President of the General Assembly on reforms of the international financial and monetary system*, United Nations, New York, 19 Mar 2009; '"G192" only credible body to bring about reforms', South North Development Monitor, no. 6655, Geneva, 9 Mar 2009.

Action, contacts and resources

International

ATTAC
www.attac.org

BankTrack
www.banktrack.org

Bretton Woods Project
www.brettonwoodsproject.org

Carbon Trade Watch
www.carbontradewatch.org

Centre on Housing Rights and
Evictions
www.cohre.org

Commission of Experts of the
President of the UN General
Assembly on Reforms of the
International Monetary and
Financial System
http://tinyurl.com/cp3w5k

Corporate Europe Observatory
www.corporateeurope.org

Corporate Watch
www.corporatewatch.org

EcoEquity
www.ecoequity.org

Eurodad
www.eurodad.org

Focus on the Global South
www.focusweb.org

Global Commons Institute
www.gci.org.uk

IFIwatchnet
www.ifiwatchnet.org

Indigenous Peoples and Reducing
Emissions from Deforestation &
Degradation (REDD)
http://thereddsite.wordpress.com

International Labour
Organization (Financial Crisis)
http://tinyurl.com/ku8q5j

International Trade Union
Confederation
www.ituc-csi-org

Jubilee Debt Campaign
www.jubileedebtcampaign.org.uk

Kyoto2
www.kyoto2.org

La Via Campesina
www.viacampesina.org

New Economics Foundation
www.neweconomics.org

Put People First
www.putpeoplefirst.org.uk

REDD-Monitor
www.redd-monitor.org

Rethinking Finance
www.rethinkingfinance.org

Southern Africa Resource Watch
www.sarwatch.org

Tax Justice Network
www.taxjustice.net

The Corner House
www.thecornerhouse.org.uk

Transition Towns
www. transitiontowns.org

Transnational Institute
www.tni.org

UN Environment Programme
(Climate Change)
www.unep.org/climatechange

War on Want
www.waronwant.org

World Development Movement
www.wdm.org.uk

National campaigns for climate justice

Australia

Climate Movement
www.climatemovement.org.au

Rising Tide
www.risingtide.org.au

Britain

Climate Camp
www.climatecamp.org.uk

Christian Aid
www. christian-aid.org.uk

Friends of the Earth UK
www.foe.co.uk

No New Coal
www.nonewcoal.org.uk

Plane Stupid
www.planestupid.org

Rising Tide
www.risingtide.org.uk

Canada

Stop Climate Chaos Coalition
www.climatechaos.net

New Zealand / Aotearoa

Climate Camp
www.climatecamp.org.nz

Save Happy Valley
www.savehappyvalley.org.nz

United States

Climate Action
www.climateaction09.org

Climate Convergence
www.climateconvergence.org

Energy Action Coalition
www.energyactioncoalition.org

Energy Justice
www.energyjustice.net

Rising Tide
www.risingtidenorthamerica.org

MAGAZINES/BLOGS

Ann Pettifor's blog on the
financial crisis
www.debtonation.org

Foreign Policy In Focus
www.fpif.org

Grist Magazine
www.grist.org

New Internationalist
www.newint.org

Z Magazine and Znet
www.zmag.org

BOOKS (Post-meltdown)

Barbara Ehrenreich, *This Land is Their Land: reports from a divided nation*, Metropolitan Books, 2008.

Larry Elliott and Dan Atkinson, *The Gods that Failed: how blind faith in markets has cost us our future*, Bodley Head, London, 2008

Mark Engler, *How to Rule the World: the coming battle over the global economy*, Nation Books, 2008.

Naomi Klein, *The Shock Doctrine: the rise of disaster capitalism*, Metropolitan Books, New York, 2008.

Paul Mason, *Meltdown: the end of the age of greed*, Verso, London, 2009.

Peter Stalker, *The No-Nonsense Guide to Global Finance*, New Internationalist Publications, Oxford, 2009.

Graham Turner, *The Credit Crunch: housing bubbles, globalisation and the worldwide economic crisis*, Pluto Press, London, 2008.

Richard Wilkinson and Kate Pickett *The Spirit Level: why more equal societies almost always do better*, Penguin (London) & Bloomsbury (New York), 2009.

Index

About the New Internationalist

The **New Internationalist** is an independent not-for-profit publishing co-operative. Our mission is to report on issues of world poverty and inequality; to focus attention on the unjust relationship between the powerful and the powerless worldwide; to debate and campaign for the radical changes necessary if the needs of all are to be met.

We publish informative current affairs titles and popular reference, like the *No-Nonsense Guides* series, complemented by world food, fiction, photography and alternative gift books, as well as calendars and diaries, maps and posters – all with a global justice world view.

Look out for the other **World Changing** title – *Nine Lives*.

We also publish the monthly **New Internationalist** magazine. Each month tackles a range of subjects, such as Afghanistan, Climate Justice, or the Economic Meltdown, exploring each issue in a concise way which is easy to understand. The main articles are packed full of photos, charts and graphs and each magazine also contains music, film and book reviews, country profiles, interviews and news.

To find out more about the New Internationalist, subscribe to the magazine, or buy any of our books take a look at: www.newint.org